Journalism and Social Media in Africa

Through innovative research studies and expert commentaries, this book documents the fast evolving invention of the relationship between the millions of social media and mobile phone users around Africa and traditional purveyors of news. Whilst social media demonstrates an unprecedented ability for the politically engaged to both bypass and influence traditional information flows, it also faces unique circumstances throughout much of Africa. Signs of social change brought by mobile technology are evident around the continent, raising questions about the nature of information exchange and citizenship.

Working from a wide variety of perspectives and methodologies, the contributors to this collection address key questions emerging from rapid communication change in Africa. The volume reveals how new, participatory, interactive communication technologies are enabling new telling's of Africa's stories.

This book was originally published as a special issue of *Ecquid Novi: African Journalism Studies*.

Chris Paterson is a senior lecturer and leader of the MA in International Communication at the School of Media and Communication at the University of Leeds, UK. He has published extensively on news agencies, international journalism and communication in Africa.

Journalism and Social Media in Africa

Studies in Innovation and Transformation

Edited by
Chris Paterson

Routledge
Taylor & Francis Group

LONDON AND NEW YORK

First published 2015
by Routledge
2 Park Square, Milton Park, Abingdon, Oxon, OX14 4RN, UK

and by Routledge
605 Third Avenue, New York, NY 10017

First issued in paperback 2020

Routledge is an imprint of the Taylor & Francis Group, an informa business

British Library Cataloguing in Publication Data
A catalogue record for this book is available from the British Library

Typeset in Times New Roman
by RefineCatch Limited, Bungay, Suffolk

Publisher's Note
The publisher accepts responsibility for any inconsistencies that may have
arisen during the conversion of this book from journal articles to book chapters,
namely the possible inclusion of journal terminology.

Disclaimer
Every effort has been made to contact copyright holders for their permission to
reprint material in this book. The publishers would be grateful to hear from any
copyright holder who is not here acknowledged and will undertake to rectify
any errors or omissions in future editions of this book.

ISBN 13: 978-0-367-73883-9 (pbk)
ISBN 13: 978-0-415-74526-0 (hbk)

Contents

CONTENTS

Comment

Citation Information

The chapters in this book were originally published in *Ecquid Novi: African Journalism Studies*, volume 34, issue 9 (February 2013). When citing this material, please use the original page numbering for each article, as follows:

Chapter 1
Editorial Note: Journalism and social media in the African context
Chris Paterson
Ecquid Novi: African Journalism Studies, volume 34, issue 9 (February 2013) pp. 1–6

Chapter 2
Challenging hegemonic media practices: Of 'alternative' media and Nigeria's democracy
Motilola Olufenwa Akinfemisoye
Ecquid Novi: African Journalism Studies, volume 34, issue 9 (February 2013) pp. 7–20

Chapter 3
Poke me, I'm a journalist: The impact of Facebook and Twitter on newsroom routines and cultures at two South African weeklies
Marenet Jordaan
Ecquid Novi: African Journalism Studies, volume 34, issue 9 (February 2013) pp. 21–35

Chapter 4
The Nairobi Hub: Emerging patterns of how foreign correspondents frame citizen journalists and social media
Paulo Nuno Vicente
Ecquid Novi: African Journalism Studies, volume 34, issue 9 (February 2013) pp. 36–49

Chapter 5
Media representations of technology in Egypt's 2011 pro-democracy protests
Melissa Loudon and B. Theo Mazumdar
Ecquid Novi: African Journalism Studies, volume 34, issue 9 (February 2013) pp. 50–67

Chapter 6
A forgotten tweet: Somalia and social media
Skye Cooley and Amy Jones
Ecquid Novi: African Journalism Studies, volume 34, issue 9 (February 2013) pp. 68–82

Chapter 7

A complicated but symbiotic affair: The relationship between mainstream media and social media in the coverage of social protests in southern Africa
Admire Mare
Ecquid Novi: African Journalism Studies, volume 34, issue 9 (February 2013) pp. 83–98

Chapter 8

Case studies from southern Africa
Chris Paterson
Ecquid Novi: African Journalism Studies, volume 34, issue 9 (February 2013) p. 99

Chapter 9

Social media and journalism: The case of Swaziland
Richard Charles Rooney
Ecquid Novi: African Journalism Studies, volume 34, issue 9 (February 2013) pp. 100–106

Chapter 10

Participatory journalism in Mozambique
Chris Paterson and Simone Doctors
Ecquid Novi: African Journalism Studies, volume 34, issue 9 (February 2013) pp. 107–114

Chapter 11

Social media and the politics of ethnicity in Zimbabwe
Shepherd Mpofu
Ecquid Novi: African Journalism Studies, volume 34, issue 9 (February 2013) pp. 115–122

Chapter 12

'It's struck a chord we have never managed to strike': Frames, perspectives and remediation strategies in the international news coverage of Kony2012
Toussaint Nothias
Ecquid Novi: African Journalism Studies, volume 34, issue 9 (February 2013) pp. 123–129

Please direct any queries you may have about the citations to
clsuk.permissions@cengage.com

Notes on Contributors

Motilola Olufenwa Akinfemisoye is a PhD student in the School of Journalism, Media and Communication at the University of Central Lancashire, UK. Her current research focuses on new 'alternative' media and the institutional practices of journalists in Nigeria.

Skye Cooley is assistant professor of Public Relations at Mississippi State University and a member of the Public Relations Association of Mississippi. His research interests and previous publications focus on international relations, crisis communication, and social media.

Simone Doctors is an independent education and international development consultant. She was formerly a lecturer at the Université de Reims Champagne-Ardenne, France, and the Universidade Pedagógica, Maputo, Mozambique.

Amy Jones is assistant professor of Journalism and Speech at the University of West Alabama and serves as the faculty advisor to the weekly university newscast, 'The Tiger Pause'. Her research interests and previous publications focus on sports communication and social media.

Marenet Jordaan is an MPhil (Journalism) graduate from the University of Stellenbosch. She worked as a print journalist before joining the University of Pretoria's Journalism Programme as a lecturer in 2009.

Melissa Loudon from the Annenberg School for Communication and Journalism, University of Southern California, Los Angeles, is interested in digital activism, ICTs for development (ICT4D) and ICTs in the global South. She has also written for MobileActive.org on mobiles and social change.

Admire Mare is a PhD candidate at the School of Journalism and Media Studies, Rhodes University. He holds a Master's in Journalism and Media Studies, awarded with distinction from Rhodes University. His research interests include the intersection of journalism and social media, social movements and new media technologies.

B. Theo Mazumdar from the Annenberg School for Communication and Journalism, University of Southern California, Los Angeles, focuses on politics in the new media, with an emphasis on international affairs, public/cyber diplomacy and journalism studies.

Shepherd Mpofu has a PhD in Media Studies from the University of the Witwatersrand, South Africa and was a Staff Development Fellow at the National University of Science and Technology (NUST), Zimbabwe. His research interests include new media, memory and identity, media and elections, media representations, and media and politics.

Toussaint Nothias is a PhD student at the School of Media and Communication, University of Leeds, UK. His research intersects journalism, postcolonial and cultural studies, focusing on Afro-pessimism in the French and British elite press through a critical discourse analysis of newspaper articles, news agencies' wires and interviews. He holds a BA in Philosophy and an MA in Cultural and Creative Industries (King's College).

Chris Paterson is a senior lecturer and leader of the MA in International Communication at the School of Media and Communication at the University of Leeds, UK. He researches issues of international journalism and communication in Africa.

Richard Charles Rooney is associate professor in the Department of Media Studies at the University of Botswana, Gaborone.

Paulo Nuno Vicente is affiliated to the Center for Research in Media and Journalism (CIMJ) and teaches at the New University of Lisbon, Portugal. As a journalist and documentarian he has been working extensively in sub-Saharan Africa, the Middle East and the Americas.

Journalism and social media in the African context

Chris Paterson

Much has been written in recent years about the rise of social media (broadly speaking, those communications technologies supporting digital sharing and dialoguing), but there has still been quite limited examination of the African context, with the notable exception of the social media's role in permitting civil society actors to communicate outside of established commercial and state channels during the so-called Arab Spring (Shirky 2011); though as Loudon and Mazumdar point out in this issue, even that discourse may be, if not overstated, ill informed.

While this special issue of *Ecquid Novi: African Journalism Studies* was conceived as an opportunity to examine the implications of social media for African journalism, it became clear that in defining 'social media' and 'African journalism' narrowly, we found their connections, and the extent of comprehensive research examining those, relatively nascent. Atton and Mabweazara (2011, 668), in their overview of research into new media and journalism in Africa, observe that 'research has largely lacked theoretical and empirical grounding in terms of examining how African mainstream journalists are forging "new" ways to practise their profession in the light of technological changes in their newsrooms'. But participatory journalism, in which narrowly defined 'social media' (blogging, tweeting and the like) play an integral role, is thriving around Africa and, with it, a significant body of research is emerging, including the examples which appear here. Importantly, though, as some authors point out in this issue, even where journalists in Africa are eager to embrace social media in their work, it is usually the case that the majority of adults in their country have no access to such media.

Collectively, the research described in this issue suggests that new forms of citizenship are emerging around Africa, as a result of widespread and innovative popular interaction with new communications technologies, including social media and the adaptation of mainstream media to those trends. I am reminded as I write these words in the United Kingdom (UK), that at the 'twenty-year anniversary of text messaging' some of the technologies having the most pronounced effect on society around Africa now are deemed passé by a Northern news media always clamouring for the latest techno-trend. But SMS (short message service, or 'texting'), while not conventionally deemed a 'social medium' is, in the African context, the dominant facilitator of new modes of participatory journalism in Africa, as many researchers have described (e.g., Moyo 2009). Furthermore, as an often shared resource in Africa (Nyamnjoh 2005), it is perhaps more genuinely social than Internet-based technologies which still have little impact in Africa outside of an urban middle class with affordable and consistent Internet access.

Given its rapid and recent uptake and apparent utility for both the poor and the middle classes, the mobile phone has increasingly occupied a central position in discourse about participatory media in Africa. Over at least the last half decade there has been mounting evidence that the technology is being used, to varying degrees, by citizens to contribute to news-making and information exchange in influential ways (Mabweazara 2011; Moyo, D. 2009; Moyo, L. 2011). Bivens (2008, 119) observes that in Zimbabwe 'information sent from mobile phones makes up some of the only news coverage mainstream media organisations can acquire'. It has also become increasingly clear that a significant amount of news and comment circulates among the Internet-connected in many African countries – a plethora of blog-based conversations which reflect, and reflect upon, mainstream sources, but which also inform a particular politically engaged public quite independently of that mainstream. Moyo (2009) refers to this as the 'parallel market of information', and the short case studies later in this issue provide examples.

The social media demonstrate an unprecedented ability for the politically engaged to both bypass and influence traditional information flows, but social media use faces unique challenges throughout much of Africa, due to underdeveloped telecommunications infrastructure, limited (though rapidly increasing) extra-urban mobile access, and bandwidth limitations in many areas. There has been a rapid escalation in the number of people using Twitter to monitor and disseminate information (Smith 2012), and the use of mobile devices is skyrocketing amid massive marketing campaigns dominated by the few multinational mobile service providers.

The embrace of communications technologies in postcolonial Africa might be crudely characterised as coming in three waves. The first was the transition from colonial to post-colonial media structures which, in their turn, proved to be propagandistic, elitist, lacking in content diversity, and only marginally more democratic than they had been under colonial regimes. The second was the tidal wave of mostly imported television raining down from newly accessible satellite broadcasters in the 1990s, and the accompanying terrestrial retransmissions of that imported culture via newly privatised broadcasters; the aggressive expansion across the continent by South African satellite television; and burgeoning MMDS (Multichannel Multipoint Distribution Service, or 'wireless cable') networks in African cities. Heralded by some as a 'renaissance' and a democratisation of the airwaves, this author (1998) asked whether it was also media imperialism at best, or re-colonisation via the media sphere at worst.

While public service broadcasting was eviscerated under the rubric of liberalisation, commercial broadcasters (in radio and television) have flourished, eager to advertise to a small but fast-growing number of Africans with disposable income. Throughout those decades of change in the electronic media a print press has survived in most countries, and positively thrived in some, with widely varying degrees of independence from government, though much commentary on the African press questions the possibility of journalism making any useful contribution to democratisation when it is itself constrained by market forces. Opuamie-Ngoa (2010, 141–142) cautions:

> As opposed to the dedication with which Africa's anti-colonial press discharged its functions, a 'global village' disease called 'profit motive' derived from the economic logic of diversification and the creation of giant industrial concerns has infected the traditional watchdog role of the media ... The continent's media today seem to be at its best as proxies in the battle between rival political camps sowing hatred, cynicism, public apathy and divisiveness.

The third wave is the one with democratic promise: the rapid embrace of interactive and personal communications technologies. It is what Rønning (2009, 26) calls Africa's 'new media pluralism'. Public conversation is increasingly held apart from the discourse of mainstream newspapers and broadcasters – at times critiquing that mainstream discourse, at times supplementing it, and perhaps at times pushing professional journalists toward a broader agenda and more in-depth analysis.

Mudhai (2011) applied Beckett's (2010) UK-based conception of a 'networked journalism' to his study of the shifting nature of newspaper reporting in Kenya, suggesting that mainstream media there show signs of struggling to catch up with an active blogosphere and to remain relevant, as events are increasingly debated via social media as they occur. In research presented at the 2012 International Association for Media and Communication Research (IAMCR) conference in Durban, Kenyan newspaper journalist, Irene Awino, described an emerging focus on 'day-two journalism' at Kenya's major newspapers, where it is rare for newspapers to break stories given the increasingly rapid dissemination of, and discussion about, political news on social media; therefore the focus has to be on providing alterative angles and in-depth analysis the next day. In his study of the role of SMS messages and blogging in the 2008 Zimbabwe elections, Dumisani Moyo (2009) concludes that 'citizen journalism is not necessarily emerging as a distinct form of "unmediated" space of communication, but rather as a hybrid form, as mainstream media increasingly tap into that space as a way of creating a certain impression about their close links to the citizenry as testimony of citizen engagement'. Indeed, we might question whether new interactions between mainstream journalism and citizen journalists are genuinely participatory journalism or merely an emerging form of public subsidy for an under-resourced journalism sector – what Fuchs (2009) describes as the 'Internet gift commodity strategy', where the uncompensated public provision of content fills the web pages of commercial media.

Newspapers in even some of Africa's poorest countries have, for some time, been creatively building networks of citizen reporters to extend their newsgathering reach. George Kasakula, an editor from the *Nation* print and online newspaper in Malawi, told me how

> in 2007 our Saturday edition, *Weekend Nation*, sounded out citizen journalists from across the country to write their own stories and send them ... the results were so overwhelming that

management decided to allocate not only one page but two. Now we have a network of over 500 citizen journalists across the country sending in stories using various ICT means ... we pay them about $2 for every story or picture published to encourage them. (Pers. comm., 3 December 2012).

But with useful new professional–amateur collaborations in news production there is also a concern about the tendency in poorly resourced newsrooms to rely heavily on information which appears to hang invitingly in cyberspace, seeming to urge journalists to employ it as 'news', with little or no verification. Mabweazara has conducted some of the most extensive observational newsroom research in several African countries. He has documented a variety of important changes underway, but observed 'the ethical and professional challenges that have emerged with the use of the Internet in the newsroom, precisely the practice of "copying and pasting" material from the Internet (sometimes without attribution, verification or attempts to talk face to face with sources)', and the pasting of Facebook conversations with sources into stories (Mabweazara 2011, 61). One Zimbabwean editor told Mabweazara that the problem with journalists growing dependent on Facebook 'is that it slants your stories toward a few people who use the platform and therefore leads to journalists missing a lot of good ideas outside the networks'(2011, 64).

SMS-based citizen journalist networks offer opportunities to shift journalism away from the level of the purely urban and national political scene. A challenge will be for national journalists to avoid the kind of sensational and bizarre stories which have so long characterised the stereotypical Western view of rural Africa, and to put such networks to use bringing a serious journalism to the continent's most disenfranchised. Where was a school promised but never built? Where is medical care lacking? Many journalists trained in a Northern tradition and working for intensely commercial organisations tend to dismiss such stories as an outmoded 'development news' model of little relevance to an urban readership. Such views threaten to limit any practical value of such extended news-gathering networks.

A vital question remains the extent to which social media and new communications technologies will contribute to political change in some of Africa's less democratic countries. While most of South Africa's neighbours contributed at great cost to that country's democratisation, some still exhibit considerable popular discontent with their own governance, including those which are democratic but with dominant ruling parties, such as Mozambique, and those which are not democratic, such as the Kingdom of Swaziland. That social media and ICTs will play a key role in political resistance and change in this region is already clear, but what remains less evident is whether that process will be gradual and deliberative, or disruptive, sudden and sweeping, as in North Africa. This journal issue investigates that conundrum in two ways: Mare's comprehensive overview of the relationship between mainstream and social media in the context of protest around southern Africa is followed by a special section of brief research summaries addressing particular aspects of the nexus between new media and social upheaval in three such countries – Zimbabwe, Mozambique and Swaziland.

Much of the published research to date on participatory journalism in Africa focuses on Nigeria, Kenya, the Arab north and the English-speaking south (especially Zimbabwe and South Africa). But studies from Swaziland and Mozambique are rare; a notable exception is Salgado's (2012) research on Lusophone Africa.

Equally important, however, is the impact of social media on journalism about Africa: whether in stories told by foreign or exile news services, or the communications of non-governmental organisations interested in conveying a certain view of Africa to the public and journalists alike; or indeed, those stories projected to the world about Africa from Africa. This issue examines, in various ways, the external image of Africa, and how the relationships of journalists (African and non-African) with social media specifically, and new media generally, impact on that. Africa has long been subject to a prejudiced form of reporting which has focused almost exclusively on specific types of negative events, with little attention to long-term processes. Do social media amplify the negative or give new voice to the positive? Do they provide a new avenue to reach journalists outside of Africa directly, to facilitate more nuanced reporting, and to critique that which falls into the old 'Afro-pessimist' paradigm? (De B'béri and Louw 2011). In a final comment in this issue, Nothias addresses the case of the 'Kony2012' campaign, which set social media records for its massive worldwide viewership but provoked ire and anguish for its reinforcement of damaging stereotypes. (An especially creative response to such stereotypes in the final weeks of 2012 was the 'Radi-aid' campaign by South African and Norwegian students and artists [see http://www.africafornorway.no], designed to raise awareness of the long-term problem of stereotyping Africa amongst journalists and the public.)

Authors in the current issue take on this variety of questions, but share a common interest in how new, participatory, interactive communications technologies are enabling new tellings of Africa's stories. This issue begins with Akinfemisoye's research into the role of social media in facilitating an alternative telling of the story of social protest in Nigeria, and moves on to Jordaan's research into the routine incorporation of social media in the work of South African newspaper journalists.

Subsequent articles address several implications of social media in the story told to the world about Africa, beginning with Vicente who, as part of a larger project on the foreign correspondent in Africa, provides a glimpse of social media use by international correspondents based in Nairobi. Loudon and Mazumdar present research on the representation of social media by journalists in the case of North African revolution, while Cooley and Jones examine the use of Twitter to inform the world about African humanitarian crises. Finally, the research articles in this issue conclude with Mare's examination of social media in political protest in southern Africa, and the three short case studies from that region, all mentioned earlier.

With gratitude to the reviewers and others who have assisted, and to all who answered the call for research contributions to this issue, the editor hopes this collection will contribute to a recent but growing evidence base and will serve to inspire a greater investigation of the intersection between African journalism and fast-emerging communications technologies.

References

Atton, C. and H. Mabweazara. 2011. New media and journalism practice in Africa: An agenda for research. *Journalism* 12(6): 667–673.

Banda, F., O.F. Mudhai and W.J. Tettey. 2009. Introduction: New media and democracy in Africa – a critical interjection. In *African media and the digital public sphere*, ed. O.F. Mudhai, W.J. Tettey and F. Banda, 1–20. New York: Palgrave Macmillan.

Beckett, C. 2010. The value of networked journalism. Conference concept report, POLIS (Journalism and Society). London: London School of Economics and Political Science.

Bivens, R.K. 2008. The Internet, mobile phones and blogging. *Journalism Practice* 2(1): 113–129.

De B'béri, B.E. and P.E. Louw. 2011. Afropessimism: A genealogy of discourse. *Critical Arts: South-North Cultural and Media Studies* 25(3): 335–346.

Fuchs, C. 2009. Information and communication technologies and society. *European Journal of Communication* 24: 69.

Kasakula, G. 2012. Personal communication, 3 December.

Mabweazara, H.M. 2011. The Internet in the print newsroom: Trends, practices and emerging cultures in Zimbabwe. In *Making online news, volume 2: Newsroom ethnographies in the second decade of Internet journalism*, ed. D. Domingo and C. Paterson, 57–69. New York: Peter Lang.

Moyo, D. 2009. Citizen journalism and the parallel market of information in Zimbabwe's 2008 elections. *Journalism Studies* 10(4): 551–567.

Moyo, L. 2011. Blogging down a dictatorship: Human rights, citizen journalism and the right to communicate in Zimbabwe. *Journalism: Theory, Practice & Criticism* 12(6): 745–760.

Mudhai, O.F. 2011. Immediacy and openness in a digital Africa: Networked-convergent journalisms in Kenya. *Journalism* 12(6): 674–691.

Nyamnjoh, F. 2005. *Africa's media: Democracy & the politics of belonging.* London: Zed Books.

Opuamie-Ngoa, S.N. 2010. Functional democracy and mass media: A critique. *Global Media Journal* (African edition) 4: 2.

Paterson, C. 1998. Reform or re-colonization? The overhaul of African television. *Review of African Political Economy* 25: 571–583.

Rønning, H. 2009. Introduction. In *The power of communication: Changes and challenges in African media*, ed. K. Skare Orgeret and H. Rønning, 5–25. Oslo: Oslo Academic Press, Unipub, Norway.

Salgado, S. 2012. The Web in African countries. *Information, Communication & Society*: 1–17.

Shirky, C. 2011. The political power of social media. *Foreign Affairs* 90(1): 28–41.

Smith, D. 2012. African Twitter map reveals how continent stays connected. *Guardian*, 26 January. http://www.guardian.co.uk/world/2012/jan/26/african-twitter-map-continent-connected (accessed 20 November 2012).

Challenging hegemonic media practices: Of 'alternative' media and Nigeria's democracy

Motilola Olufenwa Akinfemisoye

Abstract

The Nigerian press has played a significant role as a public watchdog, but the proliferation of new information technologies poses the question: Is journalism in Nigeria under threat and increasingly becoming a networked activity? This article interrogates the extent to which the collaboration between professional journalists and 'the-people-formerly-known-as-the-audience' is influencing institutional journalistic practices in Nigeria. Using the Occupy Nigeria protests, this study employs a combination of an ethnographic approach utilising semi-structured interviews and newsroom observations and critical discourse analysis of news texts to investigate whether other forms of 'alternative' journalisms are creating shifts in the balance of power between professional journalists and the audience.

Introduction

> Other forms of alternative media … present challenges to mainstream journalism,
> they challenge the exclusive authority and expertise of professional journalists
> – Atton 2007, 17

On 1 January 2012, the Nigerian government announced the removal of the fuel subsidy, resulting in a 120 per cent increase in the pump price of petrol per litre. This announcement kindled unprecedented days of protests, the first of their kind, in many cities across Nigeria. Citizens of Africa's most populous country and the largest producer of crude oil not only took to the streets of major towns and cities, but also *occupied* the social media trending on the #Occupy Nigeria hashtag on Twitter, as well as on Facebook, among other social networking sites and blogs. Compared to the Arab Spring, the Occupy Nigeria protests did not last as long, but will not be forgotten in a hurry. Dubbed 'Nigeria's Harmattan' (Ifejika 2012), Nigerians were not only reacting to the removal of the fuel subsidy, but were also calling for an end to the paradoxical existence of about 70 per cent of the country's citizens who, despite living in an oil-rich nation, subsist below the poverty line. These protests were not only tweeted and facebooked, but were also reported by Nigeria's mainstream media and the global media.

For some observers, Occupy Nigeria became a litmus test to check whether Nigerians could replicate what happened in Tunisia and Egypt. But Occupy Nigeria, unlike the Occupy movements associated with Hardt, Negri or Graeber's schools of thought and which have roots in Leftist politics, was not an attack on capitalism. Rather, it represented the appropriation of symbols which were subsequently localised to meet local demands. Occupy Nigeria protested against the political situation in Nigeria at a time when many saw the increase in the pump price of fuel as a way of furthering the prevailing economic hardship. Can it therefore be said that the Internet provided avenues for Nigerians to challenge dominant discourses on how the Occupy Nigeria protests were reported? Is there evidence that the Internet may help Nigeria actualise its democratisation project? Many academics regard the Internet as having the potential to take over the role of the press, dethrone autocratic governments, and advance the course of democracy (Megenta 2011, 7). While some argue that new media can play significant roles in sustaining democracy, others opine that new media and democracy remain strange bedfellows. Moyo (2010), for instance, provides empirical evidence from the 2008 Zimbabwean elections to suggest that the new media facilitate democracy by acting as 'monitors of democracy'. Loader and Mercea (2011, 758), however, question whether claims about the Internet's democratic potentials 'offer new opportunities for challenging dominant discourses and privileged positions of power'. Sunstein (2001) concurs that having the audience report their versions of reality will result in them consuming only those stories they want to see or hear. He notes that the Internet and all forms of 'alternative' news production wreak havoc on democracies. Fenton (2008, 238), too, advances this argument by pointing out that although the Internet offers a space for mobilisation, its potential to encourage democracy 'is not dependent on its primary features of interactivity, multiplicity and polycentrality, which are often celebrated and heralded as offering intrinsic democratic benefit'.

In discussing the media scene in Nigeria *vis-à-vis* the activities of 'alternative' journalisms, a cursory look at how it evolved and where it stands today is pertinent. The history of the Nigerian press predates the country's political history, which started with the birth of the *Iwe Irohin fun awon ara Egba ati Yoruba* in 1859. Subsequently established newspapers took a nationalist stance against the colonial powers until 1960, when Nigeria gained independence from Britain. Thereafter, the government-owned media became extended mouthpieces for government agendas, but the newspapers – which were largely privately owned – continued to champion the rights of all Nigerians.

By the early 1990s the broadcast media sector was deregulated, which meant that more players could join the media stage. Although the deregulation marked a turning point in the history of the Nigerian press, it did not take long for the military regime to clamp down on the activities of journalists, with the promulgation of anti-press freedom decrees such as the *Nigerian Press Council Decree* No. 85 of 1992 and the *Newspapers Decree* No. 43 of 1993. In his book, *Guerrilla journalism: Dispatches from the underground*, Sunday Dare chronicles what he, as a journalist and newspaper editor during the 1990s, along with his colleagues, went through during the military regimes of Ibrahim Babangida and Sani Abacha, when many were imprisoned without trial and some went into exile. In the face of repressive promulgations, and the assassination and imprisonment of journalists (especially between 1995 and 1998), the media made tortuous progress when Nigeria returned to civil rule in 1999. The local media, like their counterparts in other African countries, are 'among the forces that have shaped and continue to define the establishment of democracy' (Tettey 2001, 5). But with the presence of 'alternative' journalisms, would any counter-hegemonic discourses be useful in actualising Nigeria's democratisation project? This article seeks to examine whether any collaboration between professional journalists and the 'people-formerly-known-as-the-audience', as advocated by certain scholars, is possible in Nigeria's media sector and whether it will influence journalistic institutional practices. Using the Occupy Nigeria protests as an empirical example, this article questions whether or not journalists' reporting on the protests via tweets and other 'alternative' media platforms opened traditional journalistic gates through such reports from 'other' channels. Did that facilitate a discourse that was counter-hegemonic to those the media were used to framing?

Locating the Nigerian press within journalism literature on new media

The Nigerian media in the 21st century, like elsewhere, are said to be in a significant phase of transformation, with vast quantities of information readily available to audiences. The concomitant changes in the news production process have received substantial academic attention (Deuze 2008; Fenton 2009; Heinrich 2011; McNair 2006; Russell 2011). Media scholars have argued that journalism is currently experiencing a level of transformation not seen since the emergence of the press in the mid-19th century. In Nigeria, the widespread availability and adoption of information and communication technology (ICT) tools such as the Internet, personal computers and mobile phones, among others, has led to 'alternative' journalisms emerging. A recent survey showed that in December 2011, Nigeria had approximately 45 million Internet users in a population of 160 million (i.e. 28% of the population), compared to 200 000 users (0.16%) in 2000 (Miniwatts Marketing Group 2012). The adoption of mobile telephony has similarly been instrumental in this transformation. Of the 649 million subscribers in Africa by the end of 2011, 93 million – the highest number in Africa – were Nigerians, and technology experts predict that the figure will continue to rise (BBC News, 9 November 2011). With social networking sites, blogs and mobile phones providing alternative platforms for discourse about governance and social issues (affecting the citizenry in Nigeria as well as in other countries around the world), scholars concede that journalists operate in difficult times and that the profession is undergoing 'an identity crisis' (Allan 2005, 1; Anderson and Weymouth et al. 2007, 17). Without necessarily being a technological determinist, this author suggests that the events which shook the political elite of North Africa, the worldwide Occupy protests and especially the Occupy Nigeria protests investigated here, suggest that citizens now use new media in ways that have made 'gatewatchers' (Bruns 2008) of the audience and professional journalists, as they collectively monitor 'breaking' news.

Thus, academic debates argue whether 'alternative media have provided new spaces for alternative voices … that provide for specific community interests' (Silverstone 1999, 103). The discourse focuses on those technological innovations which are not only challenging journalism, but are also making the media converge online, where the demarcations between print, radio and television are blurring. For some scholars, Rosen's (2006) 'the-people-formerly-known-as-the-audience' have become nodes in a network structure that is impacting on the news production process (Barney 2004) and challenging the roles of journalists working in the mainstream media. Others argue that the social media are facilitating a paradigm shift in the practise of journalism. Domingo (2011, xv) remarks that 'social networks have become a source, a promotional space and an interaction opportunity between journalists and their publics, challenging the boundaries between the professional and the individual persona of reporters', while Hermida (2012, 1) concedes that 'open, networked digital media tools challenge the individualistic top-down ideology of traditional journalism'.

Although there is no unanimously agreed-on theory to describe the collaboration between professional journalists and the 'former-audience' in the news production process, academics have coined various terms to describe this phenomenon – something which serves as a starting point for this article. It has been variously dubbed 'ambient journalism', 'network journalism', 'networked journalism' and 'networked-convergent journalism' (Heinrich 2011; Hermida 2010; Mudhai 2011; Russell 2011). In describing this transformation in journalism, Hermida (2010, 300) notes that 'ambient journalism presents a multi-faceted and fragmented news experience, marking a shift away from the classical paradigm of journalism'. Fundamentally, these phrases all seem to underscore the relationship between old and new media, mainstream and alternative media – a notable rejection of the binaries that informed older scholarship on the relationship between new and traditional media.

Key thinkers of networked journalism include Jeff Jarvis, Charlie Beckett, Adrienne Russell, Ansgard Heinrich, Jessica Clark and Tracy van Slyke, among others. Russell (2011, 1) notes that networked journalism sees 'publics acting as creators, investigators, reactors, (re)makers and (re)distributors of news and where all variety of media, amateurs and professional, corporate and independent products and interests intersect at a new level'. Beckett (2010, 1) agrees that networked journalism is 'a synthesis of traditional news journalism and the emerging participatory media enabled by Web 2.0 technologies such as mobile phones, email, websites, blogs, micro-blogging and social networks'. Certain key thinkers (Arntsen 2010; Mudhai, Tettey and Banda 2009; Nyamnjoh 2005) believe that not only is there a link between the new media's interaction with mainstream media and democracy, but also that new media actually play an important role in Africa's democratisation project. Benkler (2006) puts forward a similar argument, namely that the Internet can help democracy thrive, in that it affords citizens the space to interact with one another and to participate in discourses on the public sphere.

Numerous scholars argue, however, that other forms of 'alternative' media should not be networked into mainstream media. For Samuel Freedman (2006), 'citizen journalism does not merely challenge the notion of professionalism in journalism but completely circumvents it …[and] forms part of a larger attempt to degrade, even disenfranchise journalism as practiced by trained professionals'. He advises against including citizens in the journalistic process, because 'to congratulate the wannabe with the title "journalist" is only to further erode the line between raw material and the finished product' (Freedman 2006). Freedman is, however, not alone in his views. Stuart Allan documented the reaction of several journalists and news editors after the July 2005 bombings in London. Their responses showed that they agree journalism is changing, but one interviewee commented that 'to create an open stream that's not edited is not to offer readers what we're here for. We're editors, and you've got to keep that in mind' (Allan 2007, 17). Greer and McLaughlin (2010) observe that the reports and images gathered by citizens during 'public protest [which] have the potential to provide dramatic newsworthy' materials, can be damaging to the status quo. The present study, therefore, sought to find out how Nigerian journalists handled these issues during the Occupy Nigeria protests.

Methodological approach

In gathering empirical data on what Nigerian professional journalists think of their professions given the proliferation of new media technologies and the consequences such 'alternative' journalisms have for Nigeria's nascent democracy, 36 journalists participated in this study. A combination of an ethnographic approach (using semi-structured interviews with professional journalists working for privately-owned newspapers) was used alongside newsroom observations and critical discourse analysis (CDA) of selected news texts gleaned during the Occupy Nigeria protests from the websites of two leading newspapers in Nigeria: *Punch* and *Vanguard*. Ethnography was deemed appropriate for this study because it provides an avenue for the researcher to have direct contact with the phenomenon being studied. Also, the 'identity' crisis which journalism is currently facing means that 'ethnographies of news production remain as essential as ever for explaining and understanding the complexities involved' (Cottle 2007, 1). Tedlock (2003, 165) similarly notes that 'ethnography involves an on-going attempt to place specific encounters, events and understandings into a fuller, more meaningful context'. The in-depth semi-structured interviews, which were part of the pilot study for this research, were conducted with four senior journalists who are also editors at four Nigerian newspapers. The newsroom observations were carried out in two newsrooms, to provide a basis for comparing the findings stemming from the interviews.

The newspapers (*Punch, Vanguard, Nigerian Tribune* and *Guardian*) are privately-owned national dailies with headquarters in two major Nigerian cities: Lagos, often referred to as Nigeria's commercial hub, and Ibadan, regarded as the political head-quarters of South West Nigeria (Lawal 2011). Participants were selected purposively on the basis of their journalistic experiences in terms of years on the job and professional rank. For this study, senior reporters who are also editors were sampled. Interviewing them thus provided an opportunity for the researcher to draw from the participants' wealth of experience in terms of what used to be the norm in the news production process, and the changes they now experience with the presence of new media technologies. The study sought to investigate whether or not institutional journalistic practices, in terms of news production and distribution, were still intact or had been abandoned – especially with reference to coverage of the Occupy Nigeria protests. The fieldwork was carried out between March and April 2012 – a time when security concerns about the activities of Boko Haram topped Nigeria's agenda. Subsequent events took their toll on the media, with the bombing of *ThisDay* newspaper's headquarters in Abuja in April 2012.

Further to the responses obtained during the interviews and what was observed in the newsrooms, analysis of news texts using CDA was carried out to examine whether or not the inclusion of alternative journalism materials came anywhere near challenging the existing power dynamics of the news production process.

CDA as a method of textual analysis has different approaches: the social-psychological approach (Wetherell and Potter) examines 'social psychological issues through the studying of the use of language' (Antaki et al. 2003, 2). Van Dijk, on the other hand, combines the social and cognitive approaches to CDA. He argues for the 'sociocognitive study of the reproduction of power abuse by discourse' (discourse.org 2009). For Fairclough (2010, 3), CDA's approach to analysing text is three-pronged: 'it is relational, it is dialectical, and it is transdisciplinary'. Taking this argument further is Richardson (2007, 37) who notes that 'Fairclough's model of CDA … provides a more accessible method of doing CDA than alternative theoretical approaches'. He argues that 'CDA approaches discourse as a circular process in which social practices influence texts … and in turn texts help influence society via shaping the viewpoints of those who … consume them' (Richardson 2007, 37).

Analysing texts using CDA also allows for the exploration of 'questions of power' in that 'power and ideologies may have an effect on each of the contextual levels' (Titscher et al. 2000, 151). Power in the context of this article refers to the institutional journalistic authority journalists exert in the news production process and, as such, examining how this played out in coverage of the Occupy Nigeria protests is germane to a reading of whether or not alternative journalisms were able to challenge hegemonic discourses within mainstream journalism.

Towards counter-hegemony or media predominance?

As Gramsci (1971, 12) notes, hegemony is consent which is '"historically" caused by the prestige (and consequent confidence) which the dominant group enjoys because of its position and function in the world of production'. The practise of journalism in Nigeria, as in most countries in the world, gives rise to a version of hegemonic discourse in that 'journalism does not operate outside ideology and hegemony but is deeply embedded within them' (Carpentier and Cammaerts 2007, 966). It is therefore germane to understand how journalists in Nigeria perform their institutional roles of being the Fourth Estate, especially with regard to the coverage of the fuel-subsidy-removal protests, and to unpack how power is contested and implicated in the news narrative.

The voices behind the pen

As already noted, the mainstream media in Nigeria continue to shape the country's democracy. Newspaper organisations in particular, although being more commercially oriented than independent (Tettey 2001), assume an anti-government standpoint in their news coverage, and a commercial outlook in order to attract advertisers. As such, the disposition of journalists working for newspapers tilts more towards the political economy, and this is evident in the way they covered the Occupy Nigeria protests. A senior journalist interviewed at *Punch* newspaper commented:

> *New media has opened up new frontiers and has made us as journalists more aware that the audience is very much interested in understanding Nigeria's political situation. During the Occupy Nigeria protests, I sent out journalists to various 'squares' where the protests were taking place. They spoke with the protesters and that served as a scoop for us to do more interpretive journalism. That resulted into more sales for our newspaper because many people wanted to understand why the government decided to remove the fuel subsidy.*

Coverage of the activities of 'alternative' journalism practitioners during the Occupy Nigeria protests had economic implications for the mainstream media. Citizen engagement during the protests was not merely about Nigerians finding their 'voice' as citizens in a democratic dispensation; rather, the mainstream media viewed citizens' engagement with social media and other 'alternative' platforms as a commodity to be 'marketised'. An editor at *Guardian* explained:

> *The Occupy Nigeria protests provided an opportunity for us as a newspaper organisation to include the audience in our coverage. Dedicating an entire page to publish the views of our readers during the fuel subsidy removal meant that many of them not only bought copies of our newspaper but also told their friends to. We saw this inclusion as a way of widening the gates and giving our readers a sense of belonging. Our coverage of the Occupy protests took a 'newszine' format which made it more interesting and appealing for people to read.*

Jodi Dean's (2008, 104) notion of communicative capitalism aptly captures this scenario. She notes that 'communicative capitalism designates that form of late capitalism in which values heralded as central to democracy take material form in networked communication technologies'. Also buttressing the fact that journalists in recent times have adopted an interpretive style of reporting, Salgado and Stromback (2012, 146) note that 'interpretive journalism is journalism driven by themes … reducing journalists to carriers and amplifiers of sources' messages'.

Journalists working for newspaper organisations identify with the impact the other 'alternative' media exert on their institutional practices. A senior journalist at the *Vanguard* disclosed:

New media is the in-thing and everyone seems to be catching up with it. This is impacting on our journalistic practices especially in the way we report because we can't afford to report a story that has already flooded Facebook, Blackberry messenger as breaking news. New media is putting us on our toes more than anything because by the time our newspaper has gone to bed, a major story might have broken. However, alternative journalisms are helping to promote freedom of information in Nigeria by offering various platforms for news reporting. During the protests against fuel subsidy removal for instance, we incorporated reports from the people at the scenes of protests.

The journalists interviewed also expressed an understanding of their functions within Nigeria's nascent democracy. Asked whether the 'alternative' media are negotiating spaces within the mainstream media, an editor at the *Nigerian Tribune* responded:

Alternative media can only break the news while the mainstream media has the space, which for instance Twitter doesn't, to furnish the audience with information. Journalists were at an advantage during the protests because for many of our readers, the question of credibility and reliability of news sources remains important to them and as such, they would prefer to buy newspapers.

The tendency for the audience to 'trust' the judgement of journalists working in mainstream media is evident in other countries, with Hermida (2011) stating that 'Canadians still trust mainstream media, despite the rise of social media'. Notwithstanding the decline in newspaper readership which has, for instance, pushed Canadian newspaper *Winnipeg Free Press* to devise other ways of stimulating the interests of young readers (European Journalism Centre 2012), journalists believe that the power structures within the mainstream media in Nigeria remain top-down. A senior reporter at *Punch* explained:

Many people generalise events happening in the media sectors of other countries as if the situations are the same everywhere. Nigeria is a very peculiar country where many people still do not have access to electricity let alone the Internet. To then say that the activities of 'alternative' media are challenging our positions as professional journalists is baseless. Nigerians still look up to the press for their information needs. That is why journalists have a point of duty to report with integrity in order to strengthen the country's nascent democracy.

Although journalists still follow institutional practices, the activities of other 'alternative' media channels still impact on how media agendas are framed and pursued. While they claim that alternative journalisms are simply 'complementary to what we do as journalists' (Fieldnotes from interviews, 2012), some junior reporters were charged with monitoring the different social networking sites so that they could identify newsworthy trends which might serve as scoops or pave the way for investigative journalism, thereby appropriating such media into the mainstream. It was also noted that senior journalists had several social networking sites open on their computers soon after arriving at their desks, in a bid to keep up with the plethora of information citizens are privy to. One journalist noted that '[e]veryone is working harder to become more current and be the first to break news', which explains why they have become 'gatewatchers' (to use Brun's term), along with everyone else. The dailies also had Twitter feeds linked to their websites where newsworthy tweets were incorporated into the news production process.

Unpacking the news texts

The news texts analysed in this study were purposively sampled based on the inclusion of tweets and other citizen reports. A number of discourses are obvious from the selected news texts, and running through them all is an attempt at citizen inclusion in reports. *Vanguard*'s online news for 10 January 2012 had the headline: 'Day 2: Citizens report protest across Nigeria.' This suggests that the 'former audience', who traditionally waited on journalists to feed them news reports, were now the ones relaying news about the protests from their locales. This news text also gives the impression that readers are being presented with the 'raw' information of what is happening across Nigeria, as seen through the eyes of 'citizen journalists': 'Nigerians who are either participating in the ongoing protest or who are onlookers sent in firsthand information of the protest as it were in their areas. Excerpts: [sic].' This was followed by reports from 11 'citizen reporters' who sent in their stories from 11 cities across Nigeria. The images and labels which the text uses are noteworthy: Richardson (2007, 49) argues that how 'people are named in news discourse can have a significant impact on the way … they are viewed'. In this text, other than the by-lines of the individual writers (in some cases, only the writer's first name), they are collectively described as either participating in the ongoing protest or as onlookers. This reinforces the mainstream media's dominance over whose voices can be heard and how those voices are represented. Schudson (2003) observes that media organisations employ certain frames in news reporting that tend to give 'voice' to 'official' sources, and in so doing allow the status quo to go unchallenged.

Although in theory the idea of networked journalism suggests that content from the audience is included in mainstream media news reports, the dominance of the mainstream is still at play. Mumby (1997, 346) concurs that this domination occurs 'precisely in the struggle between various groups over interpretive possibilities and what gets to count as meaningful that the hegemonic dialectic of power and resistance gets played out'.

Punch, in its online news of 8 January 2012, pursued a similar path of including snippets from the social media. Published under the headline 'Social media protesters display Jonathan, Mark, others' phone numbers', this news text suggests that journalists understand how social media can be used to mobilise participants during protests (Matheson and Allan 2010, 179). However, Nigerians are here referred to as 'protesters' who have perhaps defied the rules of privacy by 'displaying' the mobile numbers of two key politicians: that of President Goodluck Jonathan and of the Senate President, David Mark. Despite this headline appearing as a way of informing readers about how social media were used during the protests, it suggests subtle disapproval for the act of publishing these numbers, as the text continues: 'These personalities were perceived to either have a hand in the policy or have links with President Goodluck Jonathan.'

Punch included tweets in this report, with direct reference to the names of those tweeting: 'one Omodunbi also tweeted, I am something, when I was young I had no shoes but now I eat with N3m every day. What am I?' During the protests the social media were awash with riddles and jokes made by Nigerians trying to find comic relief in the situation. The above quote alludes to the President's suffering as a youngster without shoes, to the affluent life he enjoys as president, 'eating' about three million naira (approx. £12 000) a day. Incorporating this sort of tweet in the news text creates the impression that the newspaper's editor understands and shares the grievances of the protesters. However, when it comes to actually publishing the supposedly 'displayed' telephone numbers, the news text reported thus: 'President Jonathan switched off his GLO number. This is his Zain line, call him – 080230020** ... Direct Action! Obasanjo rigged himself in, and imposed a sick Yar'Adua and clueless Jonathan. Now we pay for it. Call him on 080550000**# Occupy Nigeria [sic.].' The way in which these tweets are included in the news text reveals more than meets the eye: it reveals the mainstream media's resistance to Negroponte's 'Daily me' journalism, by censoring the tweets prior to publication and especially by being discreet with the telephone numbers. Including tweets in the news text also reinforces the assumption that 'editorial independence is both furthered and challenged by the increasing role of real-time publishing through platforms such as Twitter' (Bradshaw 2011, 14), making it more difficult for journalists to ignore whatever information audience members are sharing amongst themselves. This writer of the news text ended the piece as follows: 'Abubakar, a Nigerian wrote "Goodluck Jonathan is our new Fuel Haram".' Incorporating this particular tweet at a time when the activities of Boko Haram continue to be a security threat, is one example of how the mainstream media create the impression that they have their fingers on the pulse of the citizens, when in fact a critical look at the discourse within the text reveals a leaning towards resistance. Carpentier and Cammaerts (2007, 966) succinctly put it that 'the journalism profession ... [is] a field of struggle, where the hegemonic values of objectivity, neutrality or detachment are contested by counter-hegemonic journalistic projects'.

As such, the thesis of networked journalism as transcending 'collaboration between professionals and amateurs' to bring about 'a shift in the balance of power between news providers and news consumers' (Russell 2011, 1–2), can be debated here. Despite newspapers in Nigeria being aware that citizens' activities cannot be ignored in the news production process, there is still allegiance to the status quo in the way news is reported. Fairclough (1995, 204) aptly paints a picture that the products which the mainstream media sell, are 'the outcomes of specific professional practices and techniques'.

These news texts generally suggest that Nigerian newspapers, in reporting the Occupy Nigeria protest, provided an illusion or a façade of inclusivity, in order to 'marketise' their commodity – the news. They, as producers of news, sought 'new' or different angles for marketing what they produce, hoping that it would appeal to the consumers (readers) who, according to one of the journalists interviewed, 'had a sense of satisfaction seeing their names in print and even encouraged their friends and families to buy the newspaper', thus boosting sales. Newspaper publishers and editors might therefore not necessarily be inventing 'a journalism without journalists', as Deuze and Fortunati (2011, 165) argue, where hierarchies between journalists and 'the former audience' are flattening out.

Conclusion

Despite narratives about the potential of the Internet and particularly the social media being able to help citizens resist the dynamics of news production and dissemination in both government and privately-owned media institutions (Loader and Mercea 2011, 759), the findings discussed above show that this might not necessarily be the case in Nigeria. This study has shown that 'alternative' journalism can negotiate spaces within the mainstream media by providing a 'forced agenda' for them (mainstream media) to run with, as with the *Punch* story. However, the 'alternative' voices might not necessarily produce the dominant discourse, because when they do, they too become part of the problem of having staff to pay, which might imply a dependence on advertisers and politicians, in some cases. Thus, this presents a complex picture of what social media and other 'alternative' journalisms mean for Nigerian's mainstream media and the country's nascent democracy.

Although it was through 'alternative' media platforms that the Occupy Nigeria protests – a first in Nigeria's political history – saw the light of day, celebrating social media as the saviour might be premature. Liking a Facebook posting or tweeting/retweeting a post does not necessarily allude to active citizens' engagement – especially in a country such as Nigeria, where its 28 per cent Internet penetration is reflective of economic and social welfare distribution. The question remains whether networking 'alternative' journalisms within mainstream media will help develop Nigeria's democracy or create new forms of citizenships. The possibilities of Africa – and Nigeria in particular – 'tweet[ing] its way to democracy' remain problematic. This is a topic that requires on-going research.

Acknowledgements

An earlier version of this study was presented at the African Studies Association of the UK Conference, University of Leeds, 6–8 September 2012. The author acknowledges the input of George Ogola and Peter Anderson of the School of Journalism, Media and Communication, University of Central Lancashire, as well as that of the two anonymous reviewers.

References

Allan, S. 2007. Citizen journalism and the rise of 'mass self-communication': Reporting the London bombings. *Global Media Journal* (Australian Edition) 1(1): 1–20.

Anderson, P.J. and A. Weymouth (with G. Ward). 2007. The changing world of journalism. In *The future of journalism in the advanced democracies*, ed. P.J. Anderson and A. Weymouth, 17–38. Hampshire: Ashgate Publishing Limited.

Antaki, C., M. Billig, D. Edwards and J. Potter. 2003. Discourse analysis means doing analysis: A critique of six analytical shortcomings. *Discourse Analysis Online* 1(1). http://www.shu.ac.uk/daol/previous/vl/nl/index.htm (accessed 7 April 2011).

Arntsen, H. 2010. Committing journalism? A view of the Zimbabwean 2008 general elections as interpreted by Internet news cartoons. *Communicare Journal for Communication Sciences in Southern Africa* 29 (special issue): 18–41.

Atton, C. 2002. *Alternative media.* London: Sage.

Atton, C. 2007. Current issues in alternative media research. *Sociology Compass* 1(1): 17–27.

Barney, D. 2004. *The network society*. Cambridge: Polity.

BBC News. 2011. Africa's mobile phone industry 'booming'. 9 November. http://www.bbc.co.uk/news/world-africa-15659983 (accessed 20 November 2011).

Beckett, C. 2010. *The value of networked journalism.* London: Polis: The London School of Economics and Political Science.

Bradshaw, P. 2011. Mapping digital media: Social media and news. *Open Society Foundation,* reference series No. 15.

Bruns, A. 2008. The active audience: Transforming journalism from gatekeeping to gatewatching. In *Making online news: The ethnography of new media production*, ed. C.A. Paterson and D. Domingo, 171–184. New York: Peter Lang.

Carpentier, N. and B. Cammaerts. 2006. Hegemony, democracy, agonism and journalism. *Journalism Studies* 7(6): 964–975.

Clark, J. and T. van Slyke. 2010. *Beyond the echo chamber: Reshaping politics through networked progressive media.* New York: New Press.

Condit, C.M. 1994. Hegemony in a mass-mediated society: Concordance about reproductive technologies. *Critical Studies in Mass Communication* 11(3): 205–230.

Cottle, S. 2007. Ethnography and news production: New(s) developments in the field. *Sociology Compass* 1(1): 1–16.

Dare, S. 2007. *Guerrilla journalism: Dispatches from the underground.* Ibadan: Kraft Books.

Dean, J. 2008. Communicative capitalism: Circulation and the foreclosure of politics. In *Digital media and democracy: Tactics in hard times*, ed. M. Boler, 101–122. Cambridge, MA: MIT Press.

Deuze, M. 2008. Liquid journalism and monitorial citizenship. *International Journal of Communication* 2: 848–865.

Deuze, M. and L. Fortunati. 2011. Journalism without journalists: On the power shift from journalists to employers and audiences. In *News online: Transformations & continuities*, ed. G. Meikle and G. Redden, 164–177. Basingstoke: Palgrave Macmillan.

Domingo, D. 2011. The centrality of online journalism today (and tomorrow). In *Online news, vol. 2: Newsroom ethnographies in the second decade of Internet journalism*, ed. D. Domingo and C. Patterson, xiii–xx. New York: Peter Lang Inc.

European Journalism Centre. 2012. Journalists reconnect with the public at Canadian newspaper's café. http://www.ejc.net/media_news/journalists_reconnect_with_the_public_at_canadian_newspapers_cafe/ (accessed 11 May 2012).

Fairclough, N. 1995. *Critical discourse analysis: The critical study of language*. London: Longman.

Fairclough, N. 2010. *Critical discourse analysis: The critical study of language,* second edition. London: Longman.

Fenton, N. 2008. Mediating hope: New media, politics and resistance. *International Journal of Cultural Studies* 11(2): 230–248.

Fenton, N., ed. 2009. *New media, old news: Journalism and democracy in the digital age*. London: Sage.

Freedman, S. 2006. Outside voices: Samuel Freedman on the difference between the amateur and the pro. Written by Hillary Profita for CBS news. http://www.cbsnews.com/8301-500486_162-1458655-500486.html (accessed 20 November 2011).

Gramsci, A. 1971. *Selections from The prison notebooks.* New York: International Publisher.

Greer, C. and E. McLaughlin. 2010. We predict a riot? Public order policing, new media environments and the rise of the citizen journalist. *British Journal of Criminology* 50: 1041–1059.

Heinrich, A. 2011. N*etwork journalism: Journalistic practice in interactive spheres.* New York: Routledge.

Hermida, A. 2010. Twittering the news: The emergence of ambient journalism. *Journalism Practice* 4(3): 297–308.

Hermida, A. 2011. Trust in mainstream media outdoes social media. *Reportr.net.* http://www.reportr. net/2011/05/11/trust-mainstream-media-outdoes-social-media/ (accessed 10 May 2012).

Hermida, A. 2012. Tweets and truth. *Journalism Practice* 6(5/6): 659–668.

Ifejika, N. 2012. Viewpoint: 'Nigeria Spring' here to stay. BBC News, 17 January. http://www.bbc. co.uk/news/world-africa-16591389 (accessed 20 April 2012).

Lawal, T. 2011. The hurdles before Oyo's Ajimobi. http://the-politico.com/politics/state/the-hurdles-before-oyo%E2%80%99s-ajimobi/ (accessed 11 May 2012).

Loader, B. and D. Mercea. 2011. Networking democracy? *Information, Communication & Society* 14(6): 757–769.

Matheson, D. and S. Allan. 2010. Social networks and the reporting of conflict. In *Peace journalism, war and conflict resolution,* ed. R.L. Keeble, J. Tulloch and F. Zollmann, 173–192. New York: Peter Lang Publishing Inc.

McNair, B. 2006. *Cultural chaos: Journalism, news and power in a globalised world.* London: Routledge.

Megenta, A. 2011. Can it tweet its way to democracy? The promise of participatory media in Africa. *Reuters Institute for the Study of Journalism Report.* http://reutersinstitute.politics.ox.ac. uk/fileadmin/documents/Publications/Working_Papers/Participatory_Media_in_Africa.pdf (accessed 20 November 2011).

Miniwatts Marketing Group. 2012. Internet usage statistics for Africa. http://www.internetworldstats. com/stats1.htm (accessed 30 February 2012).

Mudhai, O.F. 2011. Immediacy and openness in a digital Africa: Networked-convergent journalisms in Kenya. *Journalism* 12(6): 674–691.

Mudhai, O.F., W.J. Tettey and F. Banda. 2009. *African media and the digital public sphere.* New York: Palgrave Macmillan.

Moyo, D. 2010. The new media as monitors of democracy: Mobile phones and Zimbabwe's 2008 election. *Communicare Journal for Communication Sciences in Southern Africa* 29 (special edition): 71–85.

Mumby, D.K. 1997. The problem of hegemony: Rereading Gramsci for organizational communication studies. *Western Journal of Communication* 61(4): 343–375.

Nyamnjoh, F. 2005. *Africa's media: Democracy and the politics of belonging.* London: Zed Books.

Olukotun, A. 2002 Authoritarian state, crisis of democratisation and the underground media in Nigeria. *African Affairs* 101: 317–342.

Richardson, J.E. 2007. *Analysing newspapers: An approach from critical discourse analysis.* Houndmills: Palgrave.

Rosen, J. 2006. The people formerly known as the audience. *Pressthink.* http://archive.pressthink. org/2006/06/27/ppl_frmr.html (accessed 2 November 2011).

Salgado, S. and J. Strömbäck. 2012. Interpretive journalism: A review of concepts, operationalizations and key findings. *Journalism* 13(2): 144–161.

Schudson, M. 2003. *Sociology of news*. New York: Norton.

Silverstone, R. 1999. *Why study the media?* London: Sage.

Sunstein, C. 2001. *Republic.com.* New Jersey: Princeton University Press.

Tedlock, B. 2003. Ethnography and ethnographic representation. In *Strategies of qualitative inquiry*, second edition, ed. N.K. Denzin and Y.S. Lincoln, 165–213. Thousand Oaks, CA: Sage.

Tettey, W. 2001. The media and democratisation in Africa: Contributions, constraints and concerns of the private press. *Media, Culture and Society* 23(1): 5–31.

Titscher, S., M. Meyer, R. Wodak and E. Vetter. 2000. *Methods of text and discourse analysis*. London: Sage.

Van Dijk, T. 2009. Project on critical discourse studies. http://www.discourses.org/projects/cda/ (accessed 7 April 2011).

Poke me, I'm a journalist: The impact of Facebook and Twitter on newsroom routines and cultures at two South African weeklies

Marenet Jordaan

Abstract

Despite initial misgivings about the credibility of the information disseminated on social media, mainstream journalists have gradually started to adopt these media as professional tools. This study explores whether the professional use of Facebook and Twitter influences the processes and cultures of news selection and presentation in newspaper newsrooms. According to most of the journalists from *Rapport* and the *Mail & Guardian*, the professional use of social media has not significantly altered their processes of news selection and presentation. The researcher, however, came to the conclusion that the journalists are not as immune to social media as they might think.

Introduction

The editor-in-chief of the *Mail & Guardian*, a weekly investigative newspaper based in Johannesburg, had around 21 000 followers on Twitter in October 2012. In the Twittersphere this makes him one of the most influential, and well-known, print journalists in South Africa. According to him[1] social media are a kind of natural environment for journalists.

> We are all gossipy people. [...] [Social media usage] says I'm not only a broadcaster, this is not just a one way process, you don't have to just listen to what I have to say, I am responsive, I am an engaged part of the community, I will respond if you are someone who's been talking to me for a while and has something interesting to say.

As a professional journalist, this editor has clearly embraced social media. But does his use of social media influence the way he does his job? Various industry studies have been done about whether journalists use social media. However, academic research about how social media use might influence the daily routines and tasks of professional journalists is limited – especially within developing contexts.

This article explores whether the professional use of social media, with specific reference to Facebook and Twitter, influences the processes and cultures of news selection and presentation. To achieve this, the South African weekly newspapers, *Rapport* and *Mail & Guardian*, were used as case studies. The analysis is based on empirical research conducted at these newspapers during June and July 2011. This newsroom study, within a social constructionist paradigm, employed a combination of qualitative and quantitative research methods, including self-administered questionnaires, semi-structured interviews and direct observation.

Social researchers such as Herbert Gans ([1979]2004) and Gaye Tuchman (1978) spend years researching and studying news organisation to write their seminal works on the way journalists, for instance, routinise their work and source stories. Recently, various researchers (Cottle and Ashton 1999; Hermans, Vergeer and d'Haenens 2009; Saltzis and Dickinson 2008) have successfully proved that newsroom studies are still relevant for exploring and describing the impact of technology on newsrooms and news routines. Hermans et al. (2009, 39) have found that the Internet, for instance, has brought shifts to news flows, daily journalistic routines and professional accountability. Schultz (2007, 191) argues for a 're-invigoration' of the newsroom genre, as

> news ethnography is a key method for studying the processes and norms guiding the producers and the production, but as most of the studies are Anglo-American and were conducted around the 1970's, we need more research on the everyday processes of news work in different cultural settings in order to understand the diverse, globalised journalistic cultures of the 21st century.

While this study is limited in size and scope, it also draws on ethnographic principles, such as participant observation. Some of the fundamental principles of newsroom studies, as identified by researchers such as Gans and Tuchman, can be appreciated and adopted in context. However, this author concurs with criticism (Cottle 2000, 21) that the Gans and Tuchman approach is too narrow for a study that incorporates the flexibility of new media technologies. An alternative or critical approach to newsroom study has therefore been adopted in this research, to work within a social constructionist paradigm while incorporating Bourdieu's concept of *habitus* (1990, 56).

McQuail (2010, 68) states that critical or alternative research – as opposed to the dominant, positivist tradition – is based on a 'more complete view of communication as sharing and ritual rather than as just "transmission"'. It is within this framework that the current study adopted the social constructionist paradigm. Burr (2003, 2) describes social constructionism as 'a critical stance towards taken-for-granted knowledge'. By positioning itself within the social constructionist paradigm, this study viewed social media – as part of the interaction and communication between people – as having an influence on the creation of reality in a society. Since the focus of the study was on news production, the researcher explored how journalists experience news as a constructed reality, rather than focusing on audience perceptions.

In their research into how television journalists handled breaking news coverage of the 11 September 2001 terrorist attacks in America, Reynolds and Barnett (2003, 692) refer to social constructionism as an explanation for why journalists might rely on their 'professional experience, personal values, attitudes, and ideologies' to interpret news in a breaking news context. According to Reynolds and Barnett (2003, 692), 'within such a view journalists could quite naturally draw on professional and personal values to shape a news story, especially if the objectivity routine is no longer in place to limit this'.

Schutz (1945, 534) also argues that a person's interpretation of the world is based on his/her previous experiences of the world – a combination of the individual's own experiences and those handed down by the people from whom he/she learns. These experiences become a person's frame of reference for the future. With this in mind, Bourdieu's (1990) notion of *habitus* as a cultural indicator of future behaviour might be viewed as part of social constructionist theory.

Bourdieu (1990, 56) describes *habitus* as the 'embodied history, internalized as a second nature and so forgotten as history'. *Habitus* is not only relevant on an individual level, but also within a wider, communal context. Bourdieu (1990, 60), for instance, argues that people of the same 'class' or group (in this case journalists) are more likely to have been confronted with similar situations or events than people from different groupings.

A recent analysis by Olsson (2009) shows how the organisational cultures of three Swedish news organisations resulted in different responses and news scheduling decisions in the aftermath of the 11 September 2001 terror attacks on the United States. This is an example of a study that looks at culture, newsworthiness *and* routine within news organisations. Olsson (2009, 772) shows how Swedish Radio (SR) 'presents as an organization near obsessed with its former mistakes during prior extraordinary events. Decision making at SR needs to be understood in the context of a prevailing collective mindset of striving to not repeat previous mistakes.'

This study, in working within a critical, social constructionist paradigm, also acknowledges the role of cultural factors as contributing to how routines and practices function within a newsroom.

Newspapers: Old news?

In the context of this study it is noteworthy that newspaper journalists worldwide currently practise their craft within a climate of great uncertainty and change (Edmonds, et al. 2012; World Association of Newspapers 2011; Wunsch-Vincent and Vickery 2010). The World Association of Newspapers (2011) found that while media consumption patterns vary widely across the globe, the general trend is downwards, with daily print newspaper circulation declining by around two per cent from 2009 to 2010. It is only the Asia Pacific region and Latin America that still show some circulation growth (World Association of Newspapers 2011). In Latin America, however, newspaper advertising revenue has also declined significantly – by 23 per cent over five years (World Association of Newspapers 2011). Overall circulation of daily newspapers in South Africa has declined by 5.5 per cent annually since 2008 (Audit Bureau of Circulations 2012).

In a report for the Organisation for Economic Co-operation and Development, Wunsch-Vincent and Vickery (2010) argue that, besides competition from traditional sources such as radio and television, newspapers also have the attraction of Internet-based news sources (especially for younger readers) to contend with. The International Telecommunication Union, for instance, estimated at the end of 2011 that mobile-broadband subscriptions grew by 45 per cent annually in the four years leading up to 2011 (International Telecommunication Union 2011). The *State of the news media* report of 2011 stresses that 'the digital realm' will have a bigger influence on the future of journalism than a lack of audience or revenue will (Rosenstiel and Mitchell 2011).

While some newspapers have been suffering, social media have been thriving. This study defines social media as communication technologies that enable connections between individuals and groups where these connections lead to information-sharing and mutual influence.

In accordance with this definition, Facebook and Twitter can be viewed as social media. Facebook was established in 2004 and Twitter in 2006. Both rate amongst the ten most popular websites in the world (Alexa 2012). A 2010 study (Universal McCann 2011) of more than 40 000 Internet users in 62 countries found that 65.2 per cent of respondents manage a profile on an existing social media platform. According to this 'social media tracker' (Universal McCann 2011), people spend more hours per week visiting social media platforms and microblogging sites than they do consuming traditional media, such as newspapers and magazines.

Journalists working in traditional media institutions have not been immune to the apparent attractions of social media. A number of industry reports (Cision 2009 and 2010; McClure and Middleberg 2009; OriellaPR Network 2012) have indicated a steady increase in the uptake of social media by journalists worldwide. Newman (2009), who has done extensive research on the adoption of social media at media institutions, believes that journalists are embracing Facebook and Twitter on their 'own terms'. According to Newman, Dutton and Blank (2011, 17) attitudes within the journalism sector, towards social media, transformed during the period 2009 to 2011. These researchers (2011, 17) believe 'news organisations have gradually worked through the dilemmas associated with social media, and have published guidelines and undertaken training programmes on how to embrace these new formats whilst protecting their principles and brands'.[2]

Despite the meteoric rise of the social media, it would be erroneous to assume that they are the cause of the pressures some newspapers are facing. However, it is worthwhile exploring the influence these media have on traditional professional journalism. The 2012 *American state of the news media* report devoted a special section to 'What Facebook and Twitter mean for news' (Mitchell, Rosenstiel and Christian 2012). The report confirms that Facebook and Twitter have become pathways to news, although 'their role might not be as large as some have suggested' (Mitchell, Rosenstiel and Christian 2012).

By describing newspaper journalists' use of the social media and the influence these media have on the culture and routines within the newsroom, the current author hopes to contribute knowledge to the debate on the opportunities presented and/or the threats posed by the professional use of social media in newspaper newsrooms.

The South African press landscape

South Africa's democratisation in 1994 has had a significant impact on the print media industry, both in terms of editorial and ownership shifts (Wasserman and De Beer 2005, 37). Before 1994, the South African media were mostly split along ideological lines that corresponded with language preference (Wasserman and De Beer 2005, 38). Democratisation resulted in a shift away from the largely white-owned mainstream media, with alternative newspapers disappearing or being taken up into the mainstream print media (Wasserman and De Beer 2005, 38). The introduction of a new constitution – the Constitution of the Republic of South Africa, 1996 – guaranteed freedom of expression. The ANC's suggestion to create a Media Appeals Tribunal has, however, threatened this freedom, as well as the self-regulatory measures of the media (Berger 2010). Efforts by the ANC to introduce a Protection of State Information Bill have also been seen as an attempt to hamper the efforts of those who 'publish secrets to reveal wrongdoing' (The sound of victory 2011).

At the moment there are four primary players in the print media market in South Africa: Media24, Independent Newspapers, Avusa and Caxton (Media Development and Diversity Agency 2009, 16). These four media corporations are responsible for producing the majority of the commercial newspapers in South Africa – 68 titles as at June 2012 (Audit Bureau of Circulations 2012). Notable exceptions are the independently owned weekly newspaper, the *Mail & Guardian*, and the recently launched daily newspaper *The New Age*.

Wasserman and De Beer (2005, 39) argue that the increasingly competitive media market post-1994 has had a detrimental effect on the local media. According to Harber (2004) South Africa, after 1994, had 'more media but a smaller range of opinion'. Wasserman and De Beer (2005, 40) state that 'broadening' the range of channels, including the Internet, for information distribution should contribute to a more open society and create a media sphere in post-apartheid South Africa with the potential to strengthen democracy.

Internet use, via broadband connections and cell phones, has steadily been on the increase amongst South Africans (International Telecommunication Union 2011; World Wide Worx 2010 and 2011). However, Internet access in developing countries, including South Africa, remains far below par compared to the developed North. According to the International Telecommunications Union (2011) only 20 per cent of households in developing countries had access to the Internet at the end of 2011, compared to 71 per cent in developing countries. The cost of broadband connections in developing countries also remains high – in many such countries more than 100 per cent of the gross monthly per capita income (International Telecommunication Union 2011).

According to the national statistical service of South Africa, around 65 per cent of households in the country had no access to the Internet in 2011 (Statistics South Africa 2012). Most people (16%) accessed the Internet from their phones, while others accessed it from home (9%) or work (5%) (Statistics South Africa 2012). According to the Grants Management and Systems Administration (GMSA) (2012), South Africa has one of the highest unique mobile subscriber penetration rates in the developing world (at 66%). The average for the developing world is 38 per cent, compared to 79 per cent for developed nations (GSMA 2012). In this country, the use of cell phones with Internet access could arguably account for the meteoric rise of social media such as Facebook and Twitter over the past few years (World Wide Worx 2012; Strategy Worx 2012). By August 2012 South African had around 5.3 million Facebook users and 2.3 million Twitter users (World Wide Worx 2012).

Since South Africa has a population of around 50 million people, this means that only a relatively small minority access the social media. These media might be fast growing and increasingly reaching rural areas (World Wide Worx 2012), but they cannot yet be seen as the media of the masses in this country.

Rapport and the *Mail & Guardian*

Both South African newspapers selected for this study, *Rapport* and the *Mail & Guardian*, have an active presence on the Internet and on the social media specifically. Although the two newspapers differ in terms of target markets and ownership, they are both distributed weekly, and have similar deadlines and production routines. Focusing on such similarities might contribute to an understanding of the local media landscape, in terms of describing how these two newspapers are reacting to the introduction of a new variable, namely social media.

Rapport was established by Nasionale Pers (now known as Naspers) in 1970. The majority of the newspaper's readers (around 85%) fall in the LSM[3] 7–10 categories (De Beer 2011). A deputy-editor of *Rapport*, who describes the newspaper's readers as '*somewhere between blue collar and white collar*', maintains that very few intellectuals read the paper.

The newspaper has a website with ample space for reader interaction, a Facebook page with (at the time of writing) around 4 800 fans, and a Twitter-feed with around 6 300 followers. Various journalists at the newspaper also have their own Twitter accounts. This level of social media interaction does, however, not match the reach of the print version of the newspaper, which, at the end of 2011, averaged copy sales of around 200 000 per edition (Audit Bureau of Circulations 2012). In 2011 it was the third biggest weekend newspaper in the country.

The *Mail & Guardian*, on the other hand, regularly sold around 40 000 copies of the newspaper per week at the end of 2011 (Audit Bureau of Circulations 2012), and has more than half as many Facebook fans. In 1985, the *Mail & Guardian* originated as *The Weekly Mail*. According to the editor-in-chief, the paper's readership is well educated, with the highest proportion of readers having tertiary or postgraduate degrees. He states that the majority of the paper's readers are concentrated in the LSM 8–10 categories, and are '*broadly speaking reflective of South Africa's population*'.

The *Mail & Guardian Online* was the first Internet-based news publication in Africa when it was launched in 1994 (see Mail & Guardian Online, About us). Although the Internet publication works closely with the print version, it has its own dedicated staff and editor. The site has an active blogging community, known as Thoughtleader, and various Twitter feeds. The personalised Twitterfeed from the *Mail & Guardian* team has more than 72 000 followers, while its Facebook page has around 29 000 fans. The newspaper, which has a strong mobile presence, launched the first e-reader (Kindle) version in February 2011.

Methodology

Despite the research mainly being qualitative in nature, a quantitative data collection method – a self-administered survey – was also employed to increase the validity of the study. The general research question posed by this study was:

> How does the professional use of social media at *Rapport* and the *Mail & Guardian* influence processes and cultures of news selection and presentation?

The study specifically studied newsroom culture, the typification of news (with the focus on the difference between hard and soft news), beat structures and the journalists' relationships with their sources.

The current author designed a self-administered questionnaire to distribute to all the news journalists at *Rapport* and the *Mail & Guardian*. Since this is a relatively new field of study, especially on an academic level, the researcher mostly relied on related industry studies, academic literature on the structuring of questionnaires, and the advice of her Master's supervisor for guidance. The final questionnaire consisted of seven pages and contained four sections, each of which dealt with a specific aspect of social media use and/or newsroom routine or culture, and how these might possibly be influenced by social media. Some questions could be answered with a simple 'yes' or 'no', but for others a variety of Likert scales were used to gauge respondents' attitudes and perceptions towards several issues. The responses were coded in such a way that a higher score meant a stronger agreement with the statement in question. The researcher captured the responses in a computer database and analysed them using the tools of the Microsoft Excel software package. To validate the findings, descriptive analyses of the results were also conducted by the Centre for Statistical Consultation at Stellenbosch University. The questionnaire was completed by 21 journalists and editors in June 2011, which amounts to a response rate of around 67 per cent.

At the end of June and the beginning of July of 2011 the current author spent a week each at *Rapport* and the *Mail & Guardian's* offices, doing observation by drawing on ethnographic research principles. During this period handwritten notes were recorded while observing the journalists at work and attending various meetings. Personal field notes and informal conversations were also recorded. All the notes were reworked into a narrative to recount the time spent at each publication and how it related to the research themes. While spending time at these two publications the researcher also conducted semi-structured interviews with a purposefully selected sample of 15 journalists and editors. Some of the main topics that were raised for discussion included: news routines, relationships with sources, beat structures, news typification and newsroom culture. The influence of social media on all these areas of newsroom routine and cultures was also discussed. The feedback from the interviews was analysed according to themes using a thematic analysis software package. The findings of all three research methods were combined and compared, to arrive at an answer to the specific and general research questions.

Results: Tracking trends and making friends

In analysing the results, the researcher was reminded of the words of Dan Berkowitz (1989, 19), who worked within a naturalistic paradigm to study a television network-affiliated newsroom for two months: 'I'll never be sure that I saw everything I should have seen, heard everything I should have heard, or even if I understood anything correctly.' Despite these misgivings, the triangulation of research methods not only increased the validity of the findings, but also the researcher's understanding of the research problem. The combination of descriptive statistical analysis with the qualitative, thematic analysis and ethnographic principles arguably supplied a more rounded picture of the topic under investigation.

Newsroom culture or *habitus*

Journalists from *Rapport* and the *Mail & Guardian* are generally well educated, with the majority having obtained tertiary degrees. The majority did not grow up with Internet access, and less than half of them had used social media prior to starting to work as journalists. However, almost all of the journalists had already established profiles on Facebook or Twitter, or both. They were usually introduced to Twitter and Facebook out of personal curiosity or through socialising in friendship circles. While these journalists might all bring their individual personal histories and experiences with them into the newsroom, it would seem that, with regard to their knowledge of computers and social media, their backgrounds are quite similar.

Journalists at *Rapport* and the *Mail & Guardian* experienced their newsrooms as open and encouraging towards the use of social media. More than 95 per cent of the journalists agreed that they were encouraged to use social media as part of their job. The argument can, therefore, be substantiated that the role of newsroom culture, or collective *habitus*, played a significant role in journalists' acceptance of social media as a professional tool.

Specific emphasis was placed on the influence of the two newspapers' editors and the way they personally adopted and employed social media. A young reporter at *Rapport* said about *Rapport*'s editor that '*when you see her, she is on that phone looking at Twitter feeds*'. An online junior sub-editor at the *Mail & Guardian* said they should start a fan page on Facebook for their editor-in-chief because of his social media following.

The lack of support for social media usage from some editors – specifically the news editor at the *Mail & Guardian* – did not seem to deter the journalists from using these media. Those journalists who took part in the study were very aware of the extent to which their colleagues used, or did not use, social media. A senior reporter at the *Mail & Guardian* said they understood

> '*there are multiple generations of journalists working at the* Mail & Guardian. *Not all of them are going to embrace social media. They just don't understand it. They don't see the point.*'

However, even journalists whose attitude to social media could be described as somewhat negative, acknowledged the possible benefits other journalists were reaping from these media. For example, the news editor of the *Mail & Guardian* at the time, who did not use social media at all, stated that the one thing the social media might be useful for, is to promote stories.

The presence of social media nay-sayers, who were definitely in the minority, did not seem to detract from the overall acceptance of social media within these newsrooms. Journalists said they felt encouraged to present ideas originating from the social media. They also never felt any restrictions when it came to the time they spent on social media at work.

Journalists at the *Mail & Guardian* indicated that they were knowledgeable about their institution's expectations of them with regard to social media use. While no formal social media policy existed at the time of this study being conducted, the journalists knew one was being developed for the newspaper, and had taken part in a workshop to discuss it.[4]

Opinions at *Rapport* were far more divided on the need for a social media policy and/or formal guidelines for professional social media use at the newspaper. One senior reporter, for instance, believed journalists should just apply 'common sense'. According to him,

> it is silly for me with too many rules to try and mould the Internet into how things must work. The whole medium innovates itself, recreates itself the whole time. [...] Your rules are going to become redundant immediately. [...] At the moment the wonder of it is that it is this free-for-all where anything goes. And I think it is cool, stick to it.

Efforts to establish a social media policy at *Rapport* seemed disjointed. Despite the lack of formal social media policies at the time of the study, the newsroom cultures or *habitus* indicated an environment where the professional use of social media would flourish without fail.

Scheduling and the typification of news

Journalists at *Rapport* and the *Mail & Guardian* actively used social media for various purposes, mainly to keep abreast of general trends in the news and in society. Especially at *Rapport*, many opened Facebook and Twitter as soon as they arrived at the office, and often kept it open throughout the day. Journalists at *Rapport* were often observed looking at social media content purely out of a sense of curiosity or fascination. A senior reporter at *Rapport*, for instance, said: '*I don't always know where the line is between when I am working and when I am just looking at trash.*' One might argue that the use of social media in this fashion constitutes a waste of time and resources, because the majority of journalists did not develop the information they accessed via social media into news articles.

Working within the social constructionist paradigm, however, it is vital to keep in mind that news and realities are constructed through human interaction and the sharing of information. It can, therefore, be assumed that the information transmitted via social media helps to create multiple realities, with the audience as co-creators. Furthermore, it can be argued that one reason why journalists have kept up with trends on social media is to stay in touch with the realities created by their audiences.[5] This enables them to better understand audience expectations and what their readers are interested in. This researcher makes no claim that the journalists in question were conscious or self-reflexive about their use of social media for this purpose. It did, however, emerge from interviews and informal conversations that certain journalists regularly kept up to date with what was being said on social media regarding topics and issues they were reporting on at that stage.

Despite the fact that the majority of the journalists at *Rapport* and the *Mail & Guardian* were seemingly immersed in social media, they do not consider these media to be a driving force in managing their personal schedules in the newsroom. For the respondents, a variety of other factors (such as finding new angles on developing events-as-news) influence the way they plan for the next few days and/or weeks. This study found no overt signs of Twitter and Facebook being used to influence the overall scheduling of events-as-news within these newsrooms. The social media were hardly ever mentioned during any of the daily editorial news conferences the researcher attended. One senior reporter at the *Mail & Guardian* stated: '*It is giving social media too much importance to say that it has changed the news agenda. It has probably had an influence, but a very minimal influence [...] It's a communication tool. It's all it is.*'

Most journalists at these two publications followed social media to gather hard news. However, they made it clear that despite the ability of the social media to break hard news, they did not see newspapers – as conduits of hard news – becoming redundant or their role diminishing altogether. In other words, they did not see themselves as suddenly only reporting and writing on soft news.

It is noteworthy that the journalists did not all agree on a clear-cut distinction between hard and soft news. Tuchman (1978, 51) argues that one of the main distinctions between hard and soft news is the fact that hard news is unscheduled and needs to be disseminated urgently, lest it lose its newsworthiness. Following this reasoning, newspapers would be hard-pressed to present hard news in light of the immediacy of the social media and other Internet-based technologies. It was also apparent that when the journalists said newspapers still cover hard news, they usually began emphasising the analysis and interpretation of current events, over traditional hard or breaking news. In fact, most stressed the need for journalists to act as interpreters and aggregators of news, especially in light of an abundance of information as presented by the Internet and social media. This researcher would argue that in the current newspaper climate, Tuchman's classification of 'developing news' is more applicable than 'hard news' – especially when contrasted with 'soft news'. Tuchman (1978, 54) argues that developing news concerns 'emergent situations'. Almost half of the journalists surveyed believed the social media helped them keep abreast of developments in the news.

Within the social constructionist paradigm, it can be argued that the journalists at these newspapers were, therefore, creating news, and, by extension, new realities, through their interaction with existing knowledge and realities, as created and communicated not only by their sources, but also by other traditional media, Internet-based technologies and social media.

Relationships with sources

Two-thirds of the journalists surveyed indicated that the social media have a 'big' or 'average' influence on their relationship with their sources. This would seem to indicate a significant shift in the reporter–source relationship. However, Facebook and Twitter were still rated last in terms of importance when compared to other sources such as documents, first-person encounters and public events. When further interrogated about this, the journalists, without exception, were adamant they only used social media to initiate contact with sources. They believed they spent most of their time communicating 'one-on-one' with sources.

However, observations made using ethnographic research principles substantiate the argument that the journalists might have had an unrealistic perception of their own actions in this regard – especially at *Rapport*. While the journalists told the researcher they gathered news by talking to people in person, the majority spent most of the week in their offices behind closed doors. This researcher makes no claim that they spent all this time interacting with sources on social media, but this observation does seem to indicate that the journalists' relationships with their sources have changed, in ways that the journalists themselves perhaps do not yet fully comprehend.

In drawing this conclusion, the researcher remains cognisant of the fact these journalists remained wary about the credibility of information disseminated via social media. A distinction must, however, be made between *information* and *sources* found on social media. In the first instance, the information is not necessarily connected to a specific, recognisable person or institution and can, therefore, not always be verified. When referring to sources, however, many of the journalists admitted to using social media – especially to contact a specific person/institution and/or to develop a relationship with that person/institution. The information supplied by such a source was arguably easier to verify and was therefore considered more credible.

The concept of story ideation is closely linked to journalists' relationships with their sources, since the more sources journalists have, the better their chances of filing a story every day (Tuchman 1978, 68). Since it is argued here that the social media have brought about a shift in these relationships, it is logical to state that the social media also contributed to story ideation at *Rapport* and the *Mail & Guardian*. Around half of the journalists surveyed stated that they sometimes (every few months) find story ideas, or follow-ups for stories, on Twitter and Facebook. Around 20 per cent reported that they often (daily/weekly) find ideas on these social media.

From a social constructionist perspective, it can be argued that the influence of social media on the journalist–source relationship also influences the way news is structured and realities are created for audiences. It would follow that journalists experience (and therefore create) a different impression of a source they interact with only via social media. The portrayal of a source who a journalist contacted only via social media might arguably be more one-dimensional than a source he/she met in person.

Various journalists mentioned that people are generally less inhibited when using social media. As such, sources might be more open to divulge information, or might just be more informal when communicating with journalists via social media. Some journalists considered this to be detrimental to their sources in terms of privacy, while others saw it as a wonderful opportunity and a new avenue for story ideation. With this in mind, it can be argued that the use of social media by journalists to interact with sources actually helps to construct personality-driven news, in a way newspapers would not have been able to do before the rise of the social media.

Conclusion

Facebook and Twitter have become a natural part of the lives (on a personal as well as a professional level) of the majority of the journalists at *Rapport* and the *Mail & Guardian*. The journalists might have viewed these media as separate from their usual activities, routines and cultures within the newsroom, but from a social constructionist point of view, this researcher would argue that being immersed in social media forced the journalists to alter the way they approached news selection and presentation, even if they did not reflect internally about it.

Overall, the journalists at *Rapport* and the *Mail & Guardian* viewed social media as supplements to their work, rather than as threats. That being said, the journalists were aware that the immediacy and reach of social media such as Facebook and Twitter challenge their traditional role as journalists. They believed that their role as gatekeepers was still valid, in terms of curating and interpreting the massive influx of information their audiences had to deal with. This researcher can, therefore, conclude that the news and realities created by the journalists of *Rapport* and the *Mail & Guardian* were influenced both directly and indirectly by their professional use of the social media.

While a limited sample was used for this study, as an exploratory study this research has opened up debate and arguably created a theoretical framework for similar academic studies in an under-researched field – especially in developing contexts. The researcher also highlighted a number of issues that indicate the need for further study, such as the ethics of social media use by professional journalists, as raised by this study.

Notes

1   The interviewees granted informed consent for their names to be used and their views attributed within the context of the researcher's unpublished Master's thesis. For wider publication their names are withheld, and interviews are cited anonymously in the reference list.

2   It is important to note that these authors write from a British perspective, with some reference to other European, as well as some North-American examples. The lack of academic research on social media use by journalists, especially within in African context, was one of the drivers for this study.

3   The Living Standard Measure (LSM) is a South African market research tool used to categorise people based on criteria such as degree of urbanisation and ownership of appliances.

4   A formal social media policy with clear guidelines on, amongst other things, attribution, personal statements and branding, was launched by the *Mail & Guardian* in February 2012.

5   Not everyone – especially in a developing context such as South Africa – has access to social media. However, this researcher would argue that this limitation does not nullify the basic principle at work here.

References

Alexa: The Web information company. Top 500 sites on the web. Updated 4 November 2012. http://www.alexa.com/topsites (accessed 4 November 2012).

Audit Bureau of Circulations. 2011. ABC 4th quarter 2011 Presentation. Updated 12 February 2012. http://www.abc.org.za/Notices.aspx/Details/19 (accessed 28 October 2012).

Audit Bureau of Circulations. 2012. ABC 2nd quarter presentation. Updated 24 August 2012. http://www.abc.org.za/Notices.aspx/Details/22 (accessed 28 October 2012).

Berger, G. 2009. The struggle for press self-regulation in contemporary South Africa: Charting a course between an industry charade and a government doormat. *Communicatio* 36(3): 289–308.

Berkowitz, D. 1989. Notes from the newsroom: Reflecting on a naturalistic case study. Paper presented at the annual convention of the Association for Education in Journalism and Mass Communication, 10–13 August, Washington, DC.

Bourdieu, P. 1990. *The logic of practice.* Cambridge: Polity Press.

Burr, V. 2003. *Social constructionism.* New York: Routledge.

Cision. 2009. George Washinghton University and Cision 2009 Social Media & Online Usage Study. Updated December 2009. http://www.gwu.edu/~newsctr/10/pdfs/gw_cision_sm_study_09.PDF (accessed 4 November 2012).

Cision. 2010. 2010 Social journalism study. Updated 10 September 2010. http://www.cision.com/uk/media-research/2010-social-journalism-study/ (accessed 4 November 2012).

Cottle, S. 2000. New(s) times: Towards a 'second wave' of news ethnography. *Communications* 25(1): 19–41.

Cottle, S. and M. Ashton. 1999. From BBC newsroom to BBC newscentre: On changing technology and journalist practices. *Convergence* 5: 22–43.

De Beer, R. 2011. Email message to the author, 1 July.

Edmonds, R., E. Guskin, T. Rosenstiel and A. Mitchell. Newspapers: Building digital revenues proves painfully slow. State of the news media, 2012. Updated 11 April 2012. http://stateofthemedia.org/2012/newspapers-building-digital-revenues-proves-painfully-slow/ (accessed 28 October 2012).

Gans, H.J. [1979] 2004. *Deciding what's news: A study of CBS Evening News, NBC Nightly News, Newsweek, and Time.* Evanston: Northwestern University Press.

Global System for Mobile communications Association (GSMA). GSMA announces new global research that highlights significant growth opportunity for the mobile industry. Updated 18 October 2012. http://www.gsma.com/newsroom/gsma-announces-new-global-research-that-highlights-significant-growth-opportunity-for-the-mobile-industry/ (accessed 31 October 2012).

Harber, A. 2004. Report from South Africa: Reflections on journalism in the transition to democracy. *Ethics & International Affaris* 18(3): 79–87.

Hermans, L., M. Vergeer and L. d'Haenens. 2009. Internet in the daily life of journalists: Explaining the use of the Internet by work-related characteristics and professionals opinions. *Journal of Computer-Mediated Communication* 15: 138–157.

Informal conversation between the author and the deputy-editor of *Rapport*, 1 July 2011, Johannesburg.

Informal conversation between the author and junior online sub-editor of the *Mail & Guardian*, 8 July 2011, Johannesburg.

International Telecommunication Union (ITU). The world in 2011: ICT facts and figures. International Telecommunication Union. http://www.itu.int/ITU-D/ict/facts/2011/index.html (accessed 6 March 2012).

Mail & Guardian Online. About us: A brief history. http://mg.co.za/page/about-us/ (accessed 14 April 2011).

Mail & Guardian Online. The sound of victory – for now. Editorial. Updated 23 September 2011. http://mg.co.za/article/2011-09-23-editorial-the-sound-of-victory-for-now (accessed 1 October 2011).

McClure, J. and D. Middleberg. Key findings from the 2009 Middleberg/SNCR survey of media in the wired world. Updated 19 February 2010. http://sncr.org/sites/default/files/Middleberg-_-SNCR-Study-Exec-Summary_0.pdf (accessed 4 November 2012).

McQuail, D. 2010. *McQuail's Mass Communications Theory.* London: Sage.

Media Development & Diversity Agency. 2009. *Trends of ownership and control of media in South Africa.* Johannesburg: Media Development & Diversity Agency.

Mitchell, A., T. Rosenstiel and L. Christian. What Facebook and Twitter mean for news. The state of the news media, 2012. http://stateofthemedia.org/2012/mobile-devices-and-news-consumption-some-good-signs-for-journalism/what-facebook-and-twitter-mean-for-news/ (accessed 19 March 2012).

Newman, N. 2009. The rise of social media and its impact on mainstream journalism: A study on how newspapers and broadcasters in the UK and US are responding to a wave of participatory social media, and a historic shift in control towards individual consumers. Working paper for the Reuters Institute for the Study of Journalism. Oxford: University of Oxford.

Newman, N., W. Dutton and G. Blank. 2011. Social media in the changing ecology of news production and consumption: The case in Britain. Working paper for the annual conference of the International Communiation Association, 29 May, Boston.

Olsson, E.K. 2009. Rule regimes in news organization decision making: Explaining diversity in the actions of news organizations during extraordinary events. *Journalism* 10(6): 758–776.

Oriella PR Network. The influence game: How news is sourced and managed today. The Oriella PR Network Global Digital Journalism Study, 2012. http://www.oriellaprnetwork.com/sites/default/files/research/Oriella%20Digital%20Journalism%20Study%202012%20Final%20US.pdf (accessed 4 November 2012).

Personal interview between the author and the editor-in-chief of the *Mail & Guardian*, 13 July 2011, Johannesburg.

Personal interview between the author and a junior reporter at *Rapport*, 1 July 2011, Johannesburg.

Personal interview between the author and the news editor at the *Mail & Guardian*, 12 July 2011, Johannesburg.

Personal interview between the author and a senior reporter at the *Mail & Guardian*, 12 July 2011, Johannesburg.

Personal interview between the author and a senior reporter at *Rapport*, 30 June 2011, Johannesburg.

Republic of South Africa. 1996. Constitution of the Republic of South Africa, 108 of 1996. http:// www.info.gov.za/documents/constitution/1996/a108-96.pdf (accessed 1 October 2011).

Reynolds, A. and B. Barnett. 2003. This just in ... How national TV news handled the breaking 'live' coverage of September 11. *Journalism & Mass Communication Quarterly* 80(3): 689–703.

Rosenstiel, T. and A. Mitchell. Overview. State of the news media, 2011. http://www.stateofthemedia. org/2011/overview/ (accessed 14 April 2011).

Saltzis, K. and R. Dickinson. 2008. Inside the changing newsroom: Journalists' responses to media convergence. *Aslib Proceedings: New Information Perspectives* 60(3): 216–228.

Schultz, I. 2007. The journalistic gut feeling: Journalistic doxa, news habitus and orthodox news values. *Journalism Practice* 1(2): 190–207.

Schutz, A. 1945. On multiple realities. *Philosophy and Phenomenlogical Research* 5(4): 533–576.

Statistics South Africa (StatsSA): Census 2011. The South Africa I know, the home I understand. Updated 30 October 2012. http://www.statssa.gov.za/Census2011/Products/Census_2011_ Pictorial.pdf (accessed 31 October 2012).

Strategy Worx. Social media growth driven by smartphones in SA. Updated 22 August 2012. http:// www.strategyworx.co.za/social-media-growth-driven-by-smartphones-in-sa/ (accessed 28 October 2012).

Tuchman, G. 1978. *Making news: A study in the construction of reality.* New York: The Free Press.

Universal McCann. Wave 6: The business of social. Social media tracker 2012. Updated February 2011. http://www.umww.com/global/knowledge/view?Id=226 (accessed 3 March 2012).

Wasserman, H. and A. de Beer. 2005. Which public? Whose interest? The South African media and its role during the first ten years of democracy. *Critical Arts* 19(1): 36–51.

World Association of Newspapers. World press trends: Newspapers still reach more than Internet. Updated 12 October 2011. http://www.wan-ifra.org/press-releases/2011/10/12/world-press-trends-newspapers-still-reach-more-than-internet (accessed 3 March 2012).

World Wide Worx. Broadband speeding ahead. Updated 17 March 2010. http://www.worldwideworx. com/2010/03/17/broadband-speeding-ahead/ (accessed 16 April 2011).

World Wide Worx. SA cellphone users embrace Internet. Updated 3 February 2011. http://www. worldwideworx.com/sa-cellphone-users-embrace-internet/ (accessed 4 November 2012).

World Wide Worx. Social media breaks barriers in SA. Updated 12 September 2012. http://www. worldwideworx.com/socialmedia2012/ (accessed 28 October 2012).

Wunsch-Vincent, S. and G. Vickery. 2010. *The evolution of news and the Internet.* Paris: Organisation for Economic Co-operation and Development.

The Nairobi Hub: Emerging patterns of how foreign correspondents frame citizen journalists and social media

Paulo Nuno Vicente

Abstract

A sizable portion of our everyday knowledge about sub-Saharan Africa comes from the work of international news reporters on the continent. The profession of foreign correspondent constituted itself around a group of privileged witnesses of history, often immersed in a mythological aura, but the emergence of digital media has established some tension around a destructuration-restructuration of the journalistic field. The rhetoric of the pro-am revolution signifies the end of an era for international journalism due to the rise of citizen journalism. This research assesses how professional international news reporters are repositioning themselves in a transforming communicative environment, and how they interpret their own occupation and the role of rising actors in the transnational mediasphere.

Introduction

International news is a significant knowledge source about the 'foreign other' that can be conceptualised as part of continuing out-of-school lifelong education (Mody 2010). The news media build important foundations to facilitate an acquaintance with and understanding of international events for opinion leaders, decision makers and the public at large. Since most people are unable to directly access international events, they must rely on media reports about particular issues, and on the frames of reference within which these gain significance (Welch 1972).

International journalism is commonly understood as the production output of news media around the world and reporting about foreign countries, frequently denoting coverage by Western correspondents of countries other than their own (Chakars 2009); it can generically be defined as the news operations of a reporter covering events outside a country (Hamilton and Cozma 2009), while using sources in foreign countries to gather informational raw material (Hafez 2007).

The contemporary field of journalism is undergoing destructuration-restructuration, with new technologies working to counter previously successful formulas. This tension is causing transformation at the heart of journalistic production: 'News production (newsmaking) remains in the hands of professional journalists while the editorial function (op-ed) is dispersed through so-called "citizen journalism" on the Internet' (Demers 2007, 29). Digital media are considered to be levelling and even lowering the distinctions between professional and citizen media (Reese 2010), which brings to mind the old argument that 'anyone sending information from one country to another is a de facto foreign correspondent' (Utley 1997, 9).

The culture of foreign correspondents: An epistemological framework

Journalists' culture has been theorised as the interaction of their *ideas* (values, attitudes and beliefs), *practices* and *artifacts* (Hanitzsch 2007). This article addresses the epistemological dimension – objectivism and empiricism – as an inquiry into foreign correspondents' role perceptions, as well as their positioning within a multidimensional network of correspondences (Vicente 2012). In this sense, journalists are not detached from cultural considerations; they belong to a specific culture and to specific professional subcultures (Ginneken 1998). The newsgathering work of these professionals has been conceptualised in an ambivalent manner: between their 'fresh eyes' on the ground where they capture what permanently stationed reporters take for granted, and their recurrent focus on 'exotic' events, without being able to portray underlying processes or follow up contexts. Foreign correspondents' work has been described as a variance of cosmopolitanism and they are amongst the most celebrated transnational migrants of our time (Hannerz 2007). Also, their work may be regarded as cultivating cosmopolitanism in their audiences.

This article distinguishes between international journalism as a main thematic frame and international news reporting as a specific journalistic subculture and occupational category associated with particular fieldwork practices, pursuing what has been called *groundtruth* (Rosenblum 2010) – frequently, but not always, translated in a specific narrative format or genre: *reportage* or *feature* – in short: a distinct *profession*. While international news broadcasting is about transmitting *to* different countries, *to* different societies, *to* different cultures (Harding 2002), this study mainly concerns foreign correspondents: international news reporters *in* different countries, *in* different societies, *in* different cultures. Despite the acknowledged differences, a bridge can be established with cultural anthropology (e.g., Beliveau et al. 2011; Boudry 2007; Hannerz 1998; Stahlberg 2006) by adapting Geertz's (1973) words, by stating that anthropologists do not study villages (places), they study *in* villages.

A rising multidimensional network of correspondences

Contemporary journalism is currently undergoing a mediamorphosis (Fidler 1997). Any evaluation of this state of flux should, however, not be exclusively observed through the lens of technological developments, but crucially through qualitative aspects of newswork and news culture (Preston 2009). The computerisation and digitisation of all sectors of society (Deuze 2011) have led to the emergence of a convergent journalism (multimedia and cross-platform), and news content seems to be increasingly deterritorialised (Berglez 2008; Robertson 1997), complex (Urry 2003) and networked (Castells and Monge 2011). The combination of technology – particularly the Internet and its graphic interface, the World Wide Web – and the emergence of 'nonconventional journalists' is transforming long-held meanings and also the implications of eyewitnessing as a journalistic keyword (Zelizer 2007).

Some authors suggest we are being confronted by the emergence of a new type of foreign correspondence (Hamilton and Jenner 2003; Livingston and Asmolov 2010). Even if not well understood, the modern elitist occupational culture seems to be challenged. Different groups have been experimenting with distinct proposals (i.e., different organisational and operational modes): *new professionals* (e.g. Global Post; Pro Publica), *citizen newsrooms* (e.g. Demotix; Nowpublic) and *aggregators* (e.g. Breaking Tweets; Global Voices Online; Ushahidi) (Zuckerman 2010, 69). A distinct media ecosystem, 'the sum of elements and relations among media or between media and their environment within [a] certain time and space' (Zheng and Wang 2008), is emerging.

Contemporary journalism culture and newswork (Deuze and Marjoribanks 2009) are clearly being compressed between tradition and change in the networked media ecosystem. Research into domains such as historical context and market environment, the process of innovation, alterations in journalistic practices, challenges to established professional dynamics, and the role of user-generated content has revealed that journalism practice and journalism studies need to reconceptualise relations between news production and reception, if desiring to make sense of the new phenomena at the heart of an online evolving information architecture (Mitchelstein and Boczkowski 2009).

The adaptation of Web 2.0 and its renewed production possibilities to newswork has paved the way for still emergent and evolving forms of mash-up journalism: the combining of resources from the social web with a journalistic purpose, thereby converging several sources and third-party contents in one new, complete service or application. These creations represent an open questioning of traditional news production principles and practices, while encouraging collaborative and cooperative work (Tejedor 2007). This new technical hybridity suggests a new social hybridity, as captured by renewed discourse on what it means to be a professional journalist, and has been condensed in the concept of the pro-am (professional-amateur): 'Innovative, committed and networked amateurs working to professional standards' (Leadbeater and Miller 2004, 9).

The pro-am considers user-generated content an informal economic activity, thus escaping conventional forms of measurement, governance and taxation, while 'not in opposition to professional or "producer media", or in hybridized forms of subjective combination with it (the so-called "prosumer" or "pro-am" system), but in relation to different criteria, namely the formal and informal elements in media industries' (Lobato et al. 2011).

The socially networked Internet (Lewis 2010) represents the transformation from broadcast to self-cast, and from here progresses to a less asymmetrical mode of communication, i.e., from an exclusively one-directional flow (one-to-many) towards a more dialogic flow.

In recent years, online social networks have emerged as a new component of journalists' work (Portillo 2011), transforming online news production in newsrooms into more collaborative work. Studies show that a collectivist, high-context communication culture is more supportive of a collaborative work environment; consequently, this approach tends to make the news accurate and comprehensible to the public (Weiss 2008). Information aggregation, for instance from social media and online comments, is now considered a central task within networked journalism (Grueskin et al. 2011). These evolving participatory avenues in newswork resemble 'produsage', a more open participation of users in the co-production of news stories, and an arguably less hierarchical structure, where revision is a continuous process (Bruns 2008). It enhances the role of active users as gatewatchers in collaborative online news production (Bruns 2005), and that of readers as gatekeepers (Shoemaker et al. 2010).

Participation is consolidating as a norm in online journalism. It is now clear that the interpretation of professional journalism as cultivating occupational control and boundary work reveals a tension between the former news culture and a mediamorphosis that potentiates more open public participation (Hermida and Thurman 2008; O'Sullivan and Heinonen 2008). Convergence also reveals its face in effecting a distinction among professional journalists, in terms of the values held by traditionalists and convergers: those who want to maintain a hierarchical and authoritative relationship with the publics/audiences, and those who argue that users should be given a more active role in newswork (Robinson 2010).

Some segments of professional journalists align the evolving features of networked journalism with a concomitant fear of losing their authority, as a journalistic value, over the agenda of public discourse (Hayes et al. 2007). Others, meanwhile, enhance 'citizen participation, which resides at the periphery of mainstream newswork, to become embraced as an ethical norm and a founding doctrine of journalism innovation' while 'altering the rhetorical and structural borders of professional jurisdiction to invite external contribution and correction' (Lewis 2010, xi).

Previous research on international journalism, mainly from the 1970s to late 90s, mainly focused on the macro (systemic determinants) and meso (organisational) levels of analysis, and how these influence the final news content. This researcher shares Boyd-Barrett and Rantanen's (1998, 3) concern about foregrounding the significance of agency 'in the theorization of processes of globalization because we believe that without a grounded understanding of agency, such theorizing tends to grow nebulous'. In other words, this study mainly focuses on the most basic level of analysis, since 'the production of mass-mediated symbol systems is the work of individuals or small groups' (Whitney et al. 2004, 399).

This research forms part of a broader and ongoing study on the transformations in international news reporting from sub-Saharan Africa, undertaken in Nairobi (Kenya), Dakar (Senegal) and Johannesburg (South Africa). The exploratory findings presented here stem from two general lines of inquiry: How do foreign correspondents perceive their own professional culture in the face of a contemporary mediamorphosis? And how do foreign correspondents interpret and frame social media and 'citizen journalists'?

This article is based on a series of in-depth interviews with 18 foreign correspondents, conducted during two weeks of research in Nairobi. Respondents ranged from staff journalists to freelancers working for international newspapers (*Daily Telegraph, El Pais, The Guardian, The Times, Trouw, TAZ, de Volkskrant*), magazines (*Time, Newsweek*), radio (Capetalk Radio, RFI), television channels (CNBC Africa, France 24, N-24 TV, NOS, Sky News), news websites (BBC News, The Christian Science Monitor, Global Post) and news agencies (AFP, AP, IRIN News, Reuters). Distinct levels of experience in foreign correspondence are involved: from veterans (15–20 years of work) to novices (0–5 years). The interviews ranged in length from approximately 40 minutes to over two hours, and were mainly focused on life histories, perceptions of work, and the particular challenges posed by digital media – particularly the Internet – as well as career expectations. All interviews were conducted in confidence, and the names of interviewees have been withheld by mutual agreement.

The aim of this research was to observe 'how members of a specific culture attempt to make themselves a(t) home in a transforming communicative environment, how they can find themselves in this environment and at the same time try to mould it in their own image' (Miller and Slater 2000, 1). For this reason, the focus here is on the dynamics of positioning: How do foreign correspondents engage with how Internet media position them within networks that transcend their immediate location, and what is foreign correspondents' epistemological stance toward the work of pro-ams?

Following Hanitzsch (2007), observations will be articulated across levels of foreign correspondents' journalistic culture, i.e., their evaluation of professional worldviews and occupational norms, and how these determine their position amongst citizen journalists. An attempt is made to assess how people who are directly involved in the transformative processes taking place within international journalism – destructuration-restructuration – consciously identify with these processes (or fail to do so), through their own interpretations and practices.

The Nairobi Hub: Among foreign correspondents

Foreign correspondents' epistemologies: empiricism and objectivism

'Nairobi is a gateway to Africa,' says A., citing the long history of the Kenyan capital as a central basis for journalists covering not only East Africa, but often all of sub-Saharan Africa and even the continent as a whole. In itself, the assertion shows how professional international news reporting from sub-Saharan Africa has translated its pursuit of empirically-based reports into an objectified justification for establishing overseas bureaus, keeping local staff journalists or paying on a piece-by-piece basis for reports 'pitched' by freelancers in the field.

Regarding 'the means by which a truth claim is ultimately justified by the journalist' (Hanitzsch 2007, 377), the professional correspondents interviewed for this study highly value empiricism – particularly observation, evidence and direct experience – as a prescriptive occupational norm for fieldwork. As H., a freelance journalist, puts it: '*You can't fully understand a context just by reading books or by reading articles. You need to be there and you need to be making connections with the people you are writing about.*' This safeguarding of 'context' and of 'making connections with the people' is also referred to by B., an international radio reporter:

> *Nothing can replace someone on the ground who is able to meet people and to feel the atmosphere. That's how the information is coming; it is not about picking the phone, calling someone that will tell you if the answer is yes or no. It's also about feeling things and seeing things.*

This search for contextualised information positions foreign correspondents as working along contact zones, 'social spaces where disparate cultures meet, clash, and grapple with each other [...] the space in which peoples geographically and historically separated come into contact with each other and establish ongoing relations' (Pratt 2008, 7–8), i.e., areas of cross-cultural exchange and contestation.

International reporters need to be aware of the historical and socio-cultural backgrounds of the societies they cover. The ambiguity of these contact zones is expressively exemplified by K., a journalist working for a major international news agency: '*All foreign correspondents are translators. That's the value of having a foreigner and not a local journalist, because they* [foreign correspondents] *can translate for people back home.*'

Reflecting on these 'global narratives that are not monolithic but pluralistic, in which cultures are not arranged hierarchically' JanMohamed (1992, 112) frames the discussion between the notions of a syncretic border intellectual, 'able to combine elements of the two cultures in order to articulate new syncretic forms and experiences', and the specular border intellectual who, 'while perhaps equally familiar with two cultures, finds himself or herself unable or unwilling to be "at home" in these societies' (JanMohamed 1992, 97).

> *Despite I'm here for so long, it's my [national] background, it's where I was raised, where I grew up, those are the glasses I'm looking at Africa. So, I can be the ears, the eyes, the nose of the people who read my newspaper here. I can help explain them what I think it's relevant for them to know because it may have not just an impact in Africa, it may well have a worldwide impact.* (Excerpt from interview with E., a veteran freelance journalist)

> *I think foreign correspondents add, for better or for worst, the narrative of what is happening to news. We take a bunch of stories and facts and – I think this may be well controversial – we produce the narrative of what is happening. I think the value that is added comes from being someone from the outside who is trying to put the pieces together in a much broader sense, step back and looking for everything, and has an editor in the [central bureau] who is doing exactly the same thing. [...] Foreign correspondence is different from being a journalist in your home country, you are two quarters reporter and one quarter columnist or analyst.* (Excerpt from interview with W., a journalist working for an international news magazine)

From these excerpts, a tension arises among foreign reporters between preserving what can be perceived as an ability to build news reports from a detached stance ('outsider perspective') and the needed personal immersion ('two quarters reporter and one quarter analyst') in order to build a body of knowledge *on* and *within* a distinct culture. In other words, 'while the rules of objective journalism prohibit reporters from making subjective interpretations, their task demands it' (Pedelty 1995, 7).

This distinctive epistemological ambiguity (the 'translation') is suggested by an attempt to balance empiricism and objectivism, where 'the observer and the observed are seen as two distinct categories, and it is assumed that reality, in principle, can be perceived and described "as it is" and tested against the "genuine reality"' (Hanitzsch 2007, 376).

Although foreign correspondents based in Nairobi strongly underline the importance of 'being there', they recognise that despite its prescriptive strength as an essential first step in what can be understood as 'quality news reporting', nowadays they often find themselves unable to honour that professional commitment:

> *In order to understand the story you have to be there. One of my focuses here is to cover Somalia. We have a tight policy when it comes to go to Mogadishu. And it's a nightmare! How am I supposed to understand Mogadishu without being able to go there? I don't know what the place looks like. I don't know the people. I can't even mentally draw the city outlines. If I did, even not being there, if a blast goes on I could write a more colorful piece.* (Excerpt from interview with L., a journalist working for a major international news agency)

> *I had to give up on fantastic stories because we just don't have the money to do them. [...] I had in the last couple months ignored deadly attacks in Northern Kenya by Al Shabaab-linked groups because we couldn't pay stringers 40 dollars to send us the story! I mean, I'm really talking about 40, 50 dollars apiece. So we ignored it. [...] Our subscribers can't pay anymore for our services and we can't charge them more, because we know they are suffering.* (Excerpt from interview with H., a journalist working for a major international news agency)

It is therefore important to note how, in daily news routines, organisational circumstances can be perceived as a noticeable constraint to the correspondents' work by the journalists themselves. In this regard, two major structural convictions, among foreign correspondents based in Nairobi regarding international news reporting, are noteworthy. The first is a general recognition of a *de facto* degradation of the economic support structure: this pattern is not only expressed by the staff of major international news media, but crucially by a large number of freelancers who struggle daily to pay not only costs relating to their work (airfare, accommodation, translator, etc.), but to sustain themselves in the profession while producing news. Second, is the acknowledgement of an ongoing (often seen as irreversible) transformation in the material basis (technological) of the profession.

Dynamics of (re)positioning: Boundary-work

Here, positioning refers to 'strategies for surviving or succeeding in these new flows and spaces' (Miller and Slater 2000, 20) that characterise the network society (Castells

1999, 2000, 2007, 2011). This study investigates whether foreign correspondents are reconceptualising their role, and departing from their interpretation of social media and citizen journalism, here theorised as a 'rupture' (Appadurai 1996) in the precise sense that developments in microelectronics 'offer new resources and new disciplines for the construction of imagined selves and imagined worlds' (Appadurai 1996, 3). In other words, a qualitative understanding is sought of how foreign correspondents position themselves within a transforming communicative environment.

In that regard, professionalism is clearly noted in foreign correspondents' self-narratives as a crucial point between who is – and, normatively, shall be kept – within or outside the profession's boundary. As previously noted, occupations claim and compete for jurisdiction over work areas (Abbott 1988; Larson 1977; Schudson and Anderson 2009), in a demarcation process which attributes selected characteristics to specific institutions – in this context, interpreted as practitioners, methods, stocks of knowledge, values and work organisation, for the purposes of constructing social boundary-distinguishing activities (Gieryn 1983; Ginneken 1998):

> *I'm a professional. I've studied and I have been trained to do this. I'm supposed to stick to some professional principles. If I am caught breaking those I can be kicked out. Otherwise, some citizen journalist who blogs, who happens to be in one place and capture something with a phone: it's information, it's the same raw material that I work with, but it's not a product in the same way [...] in the sense they are less accountable. They are just offering more raw material.* (Excerpt from interview with JM., a newspaper correspondent)

> *We still need professional observers. The problem with citizen journalists is that there are no consequences for false reporting. If I report something that is wrong I get fired. If citizen journalists report something that is wrong, so what? That's why there's no substitute for professional observers.* (Excerpt from interview with H., a journalist working for a major international news agency)

> *[It's] the difference between a guy in Somalia with a mobile phone, passing information for a wider readership and a guy in Nairobi using it ... his sources, phoning them to check them, and then sending the information on. So, it's verification, it's experience, it's legal training, it's access.* (Excerpt from interview with P., a long-standing newspaper correspondent)

> *As journalists we were trained to not even assume that your name spells like that, but to check. Even if you're having a telephone interview you have to ask the person to spell his name. But now everybody is a journalist, everybody is a photographer and they just put out the stuff. I think it really poses a real challenge. And the trap in which journalists can fall into is to use this information as if it has been verified, information that they pick up on Twitter. I even found journalists who see Wikipedia as the Bible for information. It's only supposed to be a starting point to your search.* (Excerpt from interview with A., a television journalist)

It is evident that in the process of creating a social boundary between professional journalists and citizen-generated media, formal training, technical expertise (e.g., verification methods), personal and/or institutional reputation, access and an internal regulation/monitoring system to ensure accountability are suggested as differentiating factors:

In the old days, a newspaper was a newspaper. And if you were an audience member and had something to talk about, the newspaper was closed, you couldn't get in there. And so there was a clear divide: it was on the newspaper, it was done by professional journalists. Then came the Internet, the bloggers, and the bloggers or these guys who just have opinions on stuff they talk in the Internet. But now the professional media has migrated to the Internet as well. There is no clear distinction between who is a professional journalist, who is a citizen journalist, who is a blogger, who is a crazy guy who's just talking shit at home, living in his mom's basement, watching TV all day and you can't tell who these people are. So, I think that the distinction between professional journalists and everyone else is eroding. (Excerpt from interview with M., an online new media correspondent)

Professional norms and rules not only construct a specific culture, but are also constructed and validated within that particular culture and its subcultures. It seems reasonable, then, to suggest that in the midst of uncertainty ('distinction is eroding'), professional international news reporters' symbolic system works to conserve information on/from online social networks and citizen journalists. In a transforming communicative environment, the preservation of international news reporting as a self-defined subculture corresponds to the defense of using acceptable occupational modes aimed at generating and validating information from raw material. Boundary-work among Nairobi-based foreign correspondents is rooted in practitioners' epistemological assumptions:

I did some stories on the Nuba, but it was having little attention in Twitter and the guy to follow was a guy seated in New York, who had did a lot of work in Sudan and had some contacts. That I find annoying but also instructive. If people really rely on Twitter for their news – I don't know if people really are, or if the media elite is relying on Twitter ... here's a great discrimination in the media on who is using and who is not using the media. If someone is a regular user, even if it is not on the ground, they're really more interested in promoting that person rather than promoting local news stories. (Excerpt from interview with W., a journalist working for an international news magazine)

I'm not often on Facebook or LinkedIn to find news there! 'Get out of your glass house and get out there! Meet the people. Go and buy the fruit and talk to the lady how much the petrol price went up and things like that.' Then you get a relevant view of what the country is. (Excerpt from interview with L., a senior editor working for an international news service)

Some professional reporters view the evolving features of networked journalism with the concomitant dread of losing their authority as guardians of a specific form of truth validation, as a journalistic value, over the agenda of public discourse (Hayes et al. 2007). Meanwhile, others enhance 'citizen participation, which resides at the periphery of mainstream newswork, to become embraced as an ethical norm and a founding doctrine of journalism innovation', while 'altering the rhetorical and structural borders of professional jurisdiction to invite external contribution and correction' (Lewis 2010, xi).

Innovation in professional dynamics

News innovators among foreign correspondents tend to regard journalism less as a proprietary occupation and more as an open-source practice to be shared: while actively proposing solutions to the professional-participatory tension, they look to preserve fundamental ethical principles, discard outdated practices and recognise participation as a new, normative ethical principle:

> *I have mixed feelings on this because I am a real advocate for citizen journalism from the countries they are writing about. And it's really patronizing Western media send their reporters parachuting to other countries and expect them to have the best reports. It's so nonsensical because you have this people incredibly knowledgeable, they live in the country, they know all the contacts, but they are kind of not trusted I guess, so they are often used as fixers, but actually I think they must be integrated more.* (Excerpt from interview with A., a freelance journalist)

> *Kenya only has 9pm news bulletin, so when the bulletin comes other channels have to work different angles. Because if something happens at 3 o'clock, which is very late for television, chances are it has been sent by SMS, it has been tweeted, facebooked, by so many people they all know the story. You have now the challenge to come with a different angle to the story, to make it relevant. Otherwise you sound just like everybody else.* (Excerpt from interview with N., a television journalist)

Amongst informants – particularly those who can be perceived as 'innovators' – the use of online social networks tends to be interpreted as highly beneficial for newsgathering routines:

> *I think in terms of access of information Twitter is invaluable. […] It's now my second news source after the wires But having telling you that I can't say I've got amazing stories out of it.* (Excerpt from interview with P., a long-standing newspaper correspondent)

> *We need to monitor Twitter. We increasingly get tips out of Twitter, just from reading the dialogue, we learn a lot from it. For instance, sometimes we see Al Shabaab talking about an air raid. We call our guys in Mogadishu and ask them to do their own checks.* (Excerpt from interview with L., a journalist working for a major international news agency)

> *I think that social media has given us an avenue. You know, being present, being felt, and reaching up the young and upcoming audience who is not used to the conventional way of pursuing news. […] They are very important. […] These web citizens are proving to be very important sources for news and the outputs that we have. They are really helping us. We have to admit that they are not professionals, so they break so many rules and sometimes there's the risk of defaming people. They are faceless people; we don't know who they are. So, they can get away with that very easily. I can't get away with that very easily. I'm confined by the law and regulations of the media. So we are really in our toes running to beat them in their game.* (Excerpt from interview with U., a radio and online news media correspondent)

The perception of online social networks as a new, available tool for collecting information is balanced with clear concerns about seated journalism, non-stop deadlines and 24-hour news cycles:

You can easily spend a whole day monitoring information and never write a new story, so... it's something the media world to be aware of. The information flowing is huge. I think it must be assumed that we need multiple levels of filtering. You can't be doing investigative journalism and being monitoring social media. It is impossible at all, at least do it well and I don't think there's this recognition right now on attention. (Excerpt from interview with W., a journalist working for an international news magazine)

I think things like Twitter have made this 24 hour newsroom go virtual and global, and everyone is trying to tweet news before than everyone else, regardless where you are in the world. [...] All this stuff is coming from people who may not be trained, may not have angles... all that you need is a savvy editor to pull everything together and they have the story. So, you passed from needing the person on the ground, the fixer or the stringer, a comprehensive team of 5 or 6 people at least to this one person pulling on all this stuff. Media houses, for instance in London, now bring in people whom they call 'content producers', so they are not journalists anymore. What they are doing is picking content, put it online, adding the necessary photos, editing a video, embed it on the page, putting in all the metadata, tweeting, linking and it is just like this virtual competition for who can get the most hits, I guess, individually, which is sad because newspapers are really the benchmark of quality. (Excerpt from interview with A., a freelance journalist)

Discussion

The article has presented exploratory insights into ongoing transformations in international news reporting from sub-Saharan Africa. Interviews with foreign correspondents based in Nairobi suggest some uncertainty in terms of how reporters view the future of journalism as a profession. As one informant made clear, the field is 'repositioning and we are not driving it. This is just happening to us.' Given such occupational fluidity, what partially seems to be at stake (from practitioners' point of view) is how to retain tested and acceptable 'filters' and 'translators' in international news reporting.

Even if correspondents do not necessarily frame the work of pro-ams as competition to professional news reporting – some suggest the two are complementary – very strong boundary-work is in place to try to preserve certain core foundations of the job; notoriously, its epistemological paradigm based on empiricism and objectivism.

Professional reporters strongly tend to view themselves as defenders of credible public information based on their methods of collecting and verifying facts and allegations. Concomitantly, there is a tendency from more convergent sectors to regard citizen journalism and social media as relevant partners in the process of perceiving and narrating the 'Other'.

References

Abbott, A. 1988. *The system of professions: An essay on the division of expert labor*. Chicago: University of Chicago Press.

Appadurai, A. 1996. *Modernity at large: Cultural dimensions of globalization*. Minneapolis: University of Minnesota Press.

Beliveau, R., O. Hahn and G. Ipsen. 2011. Foreign correspondents as mediators and translators between cultures: Perspectives from intercultural communication research in anthropology, semiotics and cultural studies. In *Understanding foreign correspondence: A Euro-American perspective of concepts, methodologies and theories*, ed. P. Gross and G. Kopper, 129–164. New York: Peter Lang.

Berglez, P. 2008. What is global journalism? *Journalism Studies* 9(6): 845–858.

Boudry, V. 2007. Ethnojournalism: A hybrid model of ethnography and journalism to create culturally diverse news content. Doctor of Philosophy thesis, University of North Dakota.

Boyd-Barrett, O. and T. Rantanen. 1998. The globalization of news. In *The globalization of news*, ed. O. Boyd-Barrett and T. Rantanen, 1–14. London: Sage.

Bruns, A. 2005. *Gatewatching: Collaborative online news production*. New York: Peter Lang.

Bruns, A. 2008. *Blogs, Wikipedia, Second Life and beyond: From production to produsage*. New York: Peter Lang.

Castells, M. 1999. Flows, networks, and identities: A critical theory of the informational society. In *Critical education in the news information age*, ed. M. Castells, R. Flecha, P. Freire, H.A. Giroux, D. Macedo and P. Willis. Lanham: Rowman & Littlefield.

Castells, M. 2000. *The rise of the network society. Vol. 1: The information age: Economy, society, and culture*. Oxford: Blackwell Publishers.

Castells, M. 2007. Communication, power and counter-power in the network society. *International Journal of Communication* 1(1): 238–266.

Castells, M. 2011. Network theory: A network theory of power. *International Journal of Communication* 5: 773–787.

Castells, M. and P. Monge. 2011. Prologue to the special section: Network multidimensionality in the digital age. *International Journal of Communication* 5: 788–793.

Chakars, J. 2009. International journalism. In *Encyclopedia of journalism*, ed. C.H. Sterling, 764–770. Thousand Oaks: Sage.

Demers, F. 2007. Déstructuration et restructuration du journalisme. *Tic & Société* 1(1): 29–55.

Deuze, M. 2002. Online journalists in The Netherlands: Towards a profile of a new profession. *Journalism* 3(1): 85–100.

Deuze, M. 2011. What is journalism? Professional identity and ideology of journalists reconsidered. In *Cultural meanings of news*, ed. D.A. Berkowitz, 17–32. Thousand Oaks, CA: Sage.

Deuze, M. and T. Marjoribanks. 2009. Newswork. *Journalism* 10(5): 555–561.

Fidler, R.F. 1997. *Mediamorphosis: Understanding new media*. Thousand Oaks, CA: Pine Forge Press.

Geertz, C. 1973. *The interpretation of cultures: Selected essays*. New York: Basic Books.

Gieryn, T.F. 1983. Boundary-work and the demarcation of science from non-science: Strains and interests in professional ideologies of scientists. *American Sociological Review* 48(6): 781–795.

Ginneken, J.V. 1998. *Understanding global news: A critical introduction*. London: Sage.

Golan, G.J. 2010. Determinants of international news coverage. In *International media communication in a global age*, ed. G.J. Golan, T.J. Johnson and W. Wanta, 125–144. New York: Routledge.

Grueskin, B., A. Seave and L. Graves. 2011. Aggregation: 'Shameless' – and essential. In *The story so far: What we know about the business of digital journalism*, ed. B. Grueskin, A. Seave and L. Graves, 83–92. New York: Columbia Journalism School, Tow Center for Digital Journalism.

Hafez, K. 2007. *The myth of media globalization*. Cambridge: Polity Press.

Hamilton, J.M. and R. Cozma. 2009. Foreign correspondents, electronic. In *Encyclopedia of journalism*, ed. C.H. Sterling, 596–603. Thousand Oaks, CA: Sage.

Hamilton, J.M. and E. Jenner. 2003. The new foreign correspondence. *Foreign Affairs* 82(5): 131–138.

Hanitzsch, T. 2007. Deconstructing journalism culture: Toward a universal theory. *Communication Theory* 17(4): 367–385.

Hannerz, U. 1998. Reporting from Jerusalem. *Cultural Anthropology* 13(4): 548–574.

Hannerz, U. 2007. Foreign correspondents and the varieties of cosmopolitanism. *Journal of Ethnic and Migration Studies* 33(2): 299–311.

Harding, P. 2002. Impartiality in international broadcasting. In *New news: Impartial broadcasting in the digital age*, ed. D. Tambini and J. Cowling, 65–75. London: IPPR (Institute for Public Policy Research).

Hayes, A.S., J.B. Singer and J. Ceppos. 2007. Shifting roles, enduring values: The credible journalist in a digital age. *Journal of Mass Media Ethics* 22(4): 262–279.

Hermida, A. and N.J. Thurman. 2008. A clash of cultures: The integration of user-generated content within professional journalistic frameworks at British newspaper websites. *Journalism Practice* 2(3): 343–356.

JanMohamed, A.R. 1992. Wordliness-without-world, homelessness-as-home: Toward a definition of the specular border intellectual. In *Edward Said: A critical reader*, ed. M. Sprinker, 218–241. Oxford: Blackwell.

Karim, K.H. 2002. Making sense of the 'Islamic peril': Journalism as cultural practice. In *Journalism after September 11*, ed. B. Zelizer and S. Allan, 101–116. London: Routledge.

Larson, M.S. 1977. *The rise of professionalism: A sociological analysis.* Berkeley: University of California Press.

Leadbeater, C. and P. Miller. 2004. *The pro-am revolution: How enthusiasts are changing our economy and society.* London: DEMOS.

Lewis, S.C. 2010. Journalism innovation and the ethic of participation: A case study of the knight foundation and its news challenge. Doctor of Philosophy thesis, The University of Texas at Austin.

Livingston, S. and G. Asmolov. 2010. Networks and the future of foreign affairs reporting. *Journalism Studies* 11(5): 745–760.

Lobato, R., J. Thomas and D. Hunter. 2011. Histories of user-generated content: Between formal and informal media economies. *International Journal of Communication* 5: 899–914.

Miller, D. and D. Slater. 2000. *The Internet: An ethnographic approach.* Oxford: Berg.

Mitchelstein, E. and P.J. Boczkowski. 2009. Between tradition and change: A review of recent research on online news production. *Journalism* 10(5): 562–586.

Mody, B. 2010. *The geopolitics of representation in foreign news: Explaining Darfur.* Lanham: Lexington Books.

O'Sullivan, J. and A. Heinonen. 2008. Old values, new media: Journalism role perceptions in a changing world. *Journalism Practice* 2(3): 357–371.

Pedelty, M. 1995. *War stories: The culture of foreign correspondents.* New York: Routledge.

Portillo, J.R. 2011. Redes sociales: Un nuevo entorno de trabajo para los medios de comunicación tradicionales. Paper presented at the XII Congreso de Periodismo Digital, in Huesca, Spain, 10–11 March.

Pratt, M.L. 2008. *Imperial eyes: Travel writing and transculturation.* London: Routledge.

Preston, P. 2009. *Making the news: Journalism and news cultures in Europe.* London: Routledge.

Reese, S.D. 2010. Journalism and globalization. *Sociology Compass* 3(6): 344–353.

Robertson, R. 1997. Social theory, cultural relativity and the problem of globality. In *Culture, globalization and the world system: Contemporary conditions for the representation of identity*, ed. A. King, 69–90. Minneapolis: University of Minnesota Press.

Robinson, S. 2010. Traditionalists vs. convergers: Textual privilege, boundary-work, and the journalist–audience relationship in the commenting policies of online news sites. *Convergence: The International Journal of Research into New Media Technologies* 16(1): 125–143.

Rosenblum, M. 2010. *Little bunch of madmen: Elements of global reporting*. New York: de.MO.

Schudson, M. and C. Anderson. 2009. Objectivity, professionalism and thruth seeking in journalism. In *The handbook of journalism studies*, ed. K. Wahl-Jorgensen and T. Hanitzsch, 88–101. New York: Routledge.

Shoemaker, P.J., P.R. Johnson, H. Seo and X. Wang. 2010. Os leitores como gatekeepers das notícias on-line. *Brazilian Journalism Research* 6(1): 58–83.

Stahlberg, P. 2006. On the journalist beat in India: Encounters with the near familiar. *Ethnography* 7(1): 47–67.

Tejedor, S. 2007. Periodismo 'Mashup': Combinación de recursos de la web social con una finalidad ciberperiodística. *Anàlisi* 35: 17–26.

Tunstall, J., ed. 1971. *Journalists at work. Specialist correspondents: Their news organizations, news sources, and competitor-colleagues.* London: Constable.

Urry, J. 2003. *Global complexity*. Cambridge: Polity.

Utley, G. 1997. The shrinking of foreign news: From broadcast to narrowcast. *Foreign Affairs* 76(2): 2–10.

Vicente, P.N. 2012. Remixing international news reporting: Towards a renewed confederacy of correspondences. *Central European Journal of Communication* 5(1): 61–77.

Weiss, A.S. 2008. The transformation of the newsroom: The collaborative dynamics of journalists' work. Doctor of Philosophy thesis, University of Texas at Austin.

Welch, S. 1972. The American press and Indochina, 1950–56. In *Communication in international politics*, ed. R.L. Merritt, 207–228. Urbana: University of Illinois Press.

Whitney, D.C., R.S. Sumpter and D. McQuail. 2004. News media production: Individuals, organizations, and institutions. In *The Sage handbook of media studies*, ed. J.D.H. Downing, D. McQuail, P. Schlesinger and E. Wartella, 393–410. Thousand Oaks: Sage.

Williamson, A. 2011. Driving civic participation through social media. Paper presented at the Perspectives of Web 2.0 for Citizenship Education in Europe, in Brno, 7–9 April.

Zelizer, B. 2007. On 'having been there': 'Eyewitnessing' as a journalistic key word. *Critical Studies in Mass Communication* 24(5): 408–428.

Zheng, B.-W. and J. Wang. 2008. The impact of digitization upon media ecology. *Journal of Lanzhou University (Social Sciences)* 5(004): 8–13.

Zuckerman, E. 2010. International reporting in the age of participatory media. *Daedalus* 139(2): 66–75.

Media representations of technology in Egypt's 2011 pro-democracy protests

Melissa Loudon and B. Theo Mazumdar

Abstract

News reporting on the 2011 Egyptian revolution made much of protesters' use of new communication technologies, including Twitter, Facebook and text messaging. The 'Revolution 2.0' version of events, however contested, is representative of the policy discourse on new technologies and democratisation exemplified in interventions such as the US State Department's promotion of 'Internet Freedom'. This article uses reports from Western and Arab/Middle East region news sources to identify and measure the prevalence of frames on the use of technology during the revolution.

Introduction

> Did social media create Egypt's revolution?
> – Headline, British Broadcasting Corporation homepage, 11 February 2011

The Egyptian revolution that ended President Hosni Mubarak's three-decade rule took the world by surprise. In the United States (US), attempts to explain why intelligence experts failed to foresee the events of January and February 2011 have made much of protesters' supposed reliance on decentralised organising through social media tools. The argument that the 18 days of unrest were 'Revolution 2.0', or made possible by 'Web 2.0' social media tools, has found favour in diverse quarters – from Western media to followers of Egyptian technology evangelist Wael Ghonim. At the same time, a separate school of thought maintains that applying the label 'Revolution 2.0' to the protests constitutes both a disservice to the protesters and a factual error.

Egypt's contested 'Revolution 2.0' foregrounds the value-laden nature of statements about the democratising potential of new technologies, in which are included the Internet, social media and mobile phones. As the US and other nations step up their efforts to promote 'Internet freedom', the events in Egypt – the capstone of the historic 2011 Arab Awakening – are already being deployed to provide empirical support for programmes that use new technologies to promote democracy. Recalling that all technologies '[invite] participation along highly specific paths of action' (Kallinikos 2004, 254), the 'Revolution 2.0' framing of technology as a tool for democratisation is a political act, providing support and justification for particular forms of intervention.

The news media were the primary international dialogic forum on the Egyptian revolution, characterised by technological determinism in the view of some observers. Accordingly, this article aims to identify systematic biases in reporting by examining Western and Arab/Middle East region news coverage of Egypt's 'Revolution 2.0' and investigating how these sources framed the use of technology during the protests. Data from six Western and six Arab/Middle East region news sources are analysed, before combining qualitative observations on the various treatments of technology use during the protests with quantitative measures of frame prevalence across the data set.

Background

Egypt's pro-democracy protests – 'Revolution 2.0'?

On Tuesday, 25 January 2011, thousands of Egyptians took to the streets to protest high unemployment, widespread corruption and the autocratic governance of President Hosni Mubarak (Kanalley 2011). These large-scale protests, inspired by the Tunisian coup and headquartered in Cairo's Tahrir Square, were the first of their kind in Egypt since the 1970s. The demonstrations continued for 18 days, culminating in Mubarak's unseating as president and his departure from Cairo on 11 February. Unprecedented in their mix of speed, limited bloodshed, geopolitical importance and notoriety, the uprisings brought down Mubarak's 30-year reign in less than three weeks.

Those who favour classing the protests as 'Revolution 2.0' hold that they could not have occurred without the presence of Internet-enabled technologies. Social media – which include not only social networking platforms such as Facebook, but also e-mail, text messaging and photo sharing – are often emphasised (Shirky 2011). This position has been advanced by young Arab protestors, Western politicians and commentators alike. Such individuals point out that Arabic is one of Facebook's fastest-growing languages and laud Twitter's March 2012 launch of an Arabic interface. 'Revolutionaries 2.0' note that at the time of writing there were five million Facebook users in Egypt, the most in the Arab region (Ghannam 2011). One widely interviewed Egyptian protest organiser, 30-year-old Google employee, Wael Ghonim, used a Facebook page[1] that garnered 70 000 friends and a Google Group listserv to disseminate to protestors important logistical information. Ghonim told CBS News' '60 Minutes' that without social networking platforms, 'this would have never happened' (CBS News 2011).

Several Washington politicians saw in social media a risk-free opportunity to comment on the revolution. Arizona senator John McCain (in Summers 2011), for instance, fresh from a post-Mubarak trip to the region, called social networking 'the driving force in how all of this transformed and took place'. Many commentators also embraced the Egyptian demonstrations as 'Revolution 2.0'. CNN personality, Piers

Morgan (in Rich 2011), seemed to speak for many pundits when he concluded: 'The use of social media [was] the most fascinating aspect of this whole revolution.'

By contrast, 'Revolution 2.0' skeptics argue that ascribing credit for the revolution to the demonstrators' use of technology obscures the decades of repression, poor socioeconomic conditions, and demonstrators' bravery at the core of the movement. NBC News Chief Foreign Correspondent, Richard Engel, who lived for four years in Cairo and spent considerable time among the protesters, quipped:

> This didn't have anything to do with Twitter and Facebook. This had to do with people's dignity, people's pride …. Now, the protests and the Twitter and all the social networking stuff helps … but that's not why they're out. They're out because of mismanagement and a system that has really gotten so far away from its people. (MSNBC 2011)

Those who view 'Revolution 2.0' as a mischaracterisation also point to an array of statistics that undermine the claim of Internet technologies' preeminence in the revolt. They remind us, for instance, that those five million Egyptian Facebook users at the time of writing constituted only six per cent of the country's population – even on the unlikely assumption that users did not have multiple Facebook accounts. Moreover, in 2010 fixed-line and mobile broadband subscribers combined made up only 8.2 per cent of the population, with just 26.7 per cent of the population being Internet users (ITU 2012). Several commentators noted that some of the largest protests occurred after the Mubarak government cut off access to the Internet and shut down cellular phone services. That 27 January 2011 shutdown is said to have caused a 90 per cent drop in data traffic to and from Egypt. Nevertheless, when 'tens of thousands' of people took to the Cairo streets on 1 February, they formed the largest protest in Egypt up until that point (ABC News 2011). Egypt, 'dark' for five days, was not back online until 2 February.

ICT interventions and democratisation

The use of information and communication technologies (ICTs) in protest has been widely studied, with the Internet and mobile phones receiving particular attention. ICTs can help protest movements achieve results with fewer resources (Bimber 2000), expand in novel ways once communication is free of the constraints of space, place and time (Klein 1999), and develop new forms of protest such as 'electronic civil disobedience' (Wray 1999). Mobile phones in particular can be used to mobilise extremely rapidly and respond flexibly to unfolding events (Castells et al. 2007, 184–242). At the same time, the techno-utopianism of authors such as Rheingold (2002) has been met with skepticism by Diani (2000), Bennett (2003), Tilly (2003) and others, who remain unconvinced that ICTs fundamentally change the determinants of popular mobilisation.

As appropriate to a politically charged subject of study, academic work on ICTs in protest movements has not uniformly investigated – nor recommended – ICTs as an object of intervention. However, tremendous publicity generated by the Egyptian uprising, as well as others in the region, has focused attention on the efforts of the US to pursue Internet freedom as a tool of statecraft. As Secretary of State Hillary Clinton outlined in a January 2010 Washington speech, the promotion of 'Internet freedom' abroad is now a major feature of the US foreign policy platform (Lichtenstein 2011). Clinton emphasised the freedom to access information; the freedom of citizens to converse with one another; and the rights of ordinary citizens to produce their own public media. She also made the watershed announcement that the US would fund the development of tools designed to reopen access to the Internet in countries that restrict it (Shirky 2011). New media scholar Clay Shirky (2011) has criticised this 'instrumental' approach to Internet freedom, in which Washington would deliver quick, directed responses to censorship enacted by authoritarian regimes.

Instead, Shirky (2011) argues for an 'environmental' view of Internet freedom, in which social media are considered long-term tools that can strengthen the public sphere and civil society. In this environmental view, major national shifts, including pro-democratic regime change, follow rather than precede the development of a strong public sphere. Local concerns of the transitioning country are emphasised; social media are not a replacement for real-world action, but offer a way to coordinate it.

In contrast, two main arguments undercut the notion that Internet technologies and social media substantially affect national politics. The first, stressed by authors such as *The New Yorker*'s Malcolm Gladwell, is that the technological tools are ineffective. The term 'slacktivism' has entered the discourse to describe activism with little actual investment: participants might join a Facebook group, for example, but this may not translate into participatory protest action.

A more potent argument comes from scholars such as Evgeny Morozov of the Open Society Institute and Rebecca MacKinnon of the New America Foundation. They assert that states such as China are gaining ever more sophisticated means of monitoring, interdicting or coopting the tools of new and social media. These new technologies are thus as likely to strengthen authoritarian regimes as they are to undermine them (Shirky 2011). Morozov, who warns against rampant 'cyberutopianism' in Washington and among pundits, argues against a romantic view of new technologies – that they are inherently democratic, favour the freedom-lover over the terrorist, or that they favour oppressed citizens over oppressive governments. Morozov underscores the ways in which authoritarian regimes can use the same vaunted tools of Web 2.0 to propagandise, censor, surveil and persecute their citizens (Lichtenstein 2011).

As developing US policy on Internet freedom demonstrates, dialogue on the democratising potential of new technology can and does affect foreign policy discussions. Therefore, in addition to the debate over the 'Revolution 2.0' viewpoint, news media discourse on the role of new technology in the Egyptian revolution takes up important policy considerations.

Theoretical framework

Conceptual representations of technology

In the introduction to an article on his Critical Theory of Technology, Feenberg (2005, 49), citing Marcuse, reminds us that 'the choice of a technical rather than a political or moral solution to a social problem is politically and morally significant'. Conceptualising a technology in particular ways – as instrumental, a tool without prior inscribed meaning, or as somehow embedded with particular liberal or repressive values – is a similarly political choice.

Stahl's 2008 analysis of Egyptian ICT policy demonstrates the socially conservative political choices of Mubarak's government. While Mubarak is quoted as saying the goal of ICT investment is 'a better life for all Egyptians', government or private-sector beneficiaries are in reality the target for nearly all the mechanisms proposed (2008, 166–168). The implication that ICTs will improve lives primarily through trickle-down economic benefits is an example of a modernist 'techno-economic rationality' (Avgerou 2003) frame at work. This instrumental view serves both to separate technology from the relations of capitalist production in which it is embedded, and to conceal, through technocratic representation, the political nature of technical systems (Granqvist 2005, 286).

The language of development figures strongly in Egyptian government ICT policy (Stahl 2008). As in much of the developing world, early representations of information technology were dominated by the 'digital divide' between the West and the rest (for an Egyptian example, see Hashem 2002). 'Bridging' the divide required rapid development of telecommunications infrastructure and increased spending, by both donors and government, on technology in education. E-government promised efficiency and transparency in place of failing bureaucracies and, above all, ICTs were catalysts for economic growth. Although most heavily promoted by international actors such as the World Bank (Thompson 2004), the G8 Digital Opportunities Task force (DOT force) and the International Telecommunications Union (ITU) (Avgerou 2003), home-grown ICT policies in countries such as South Africa (Moodley 2005) and Egypt (Stahl 2008; Warschauer 2003) also bear the discursive hallmarks of the digital divide.

Critical perspectives on the digital divide point out its fundamental technological determinism and the artificial binary it creates between connected and disconnected populations (Warschauer 2003). The digital divide represents a particular development paradigm in which technology is an indispensable modernising force, a condition for progress along a universal development timeline (Schech 2002). Schech points out that the association of technology with modernity is present, regardless of whether the technology being discussed is radio, personal computers or the Internet. For example, in a review of ICT for development initiatives in Egypt, Kamel (2010, 177) illustrates a position that, despite its caveat on the application of ICT, nevertheless asserts an instrumental (and economically constituted) relationship between technology and modern life:

> ICT is not an end in itself, however, but a means of reaching broader policy objectives. The main objective of ICT should be to improve the everyday lives of community members, fight poverty and advance the Millennium Development Goals (MDGs). In this respect, ICT is delivering the key productivity gains that enable lives of material comfort for many around the world that would have been unthinkable only two centuries ago.

Thus, the way technology is represented in relation to social, economic and political development is part of a particular knowledge system, reproduced by and legitimising particular exercises of power. Knowledge systems, forms of power and intervention are reciprocally confirming. Whether in the hands of international institutions, Western governments or policymakers in Egypt, development functions as 'an institutional apparatus that links forms of knowledge about the third world with the deployment of particular forms of power and intervention' (Mahmud 1999, 27). In the age of mass media, the neoliberal 'marketplace of ideas' frame was used to justify media privatisation as a tool for political development through democratisation (Curran 2000). The discourse of 'Internet freedom' and the democratisation potential of social media tools is an emerging successor. As such, it should be critically analysed with respect to the way technology is represented, and the particular 'forms of power and intervention' that are legitimated in the process.

News framing

As a demonstration of the legitimating function of conceptual representations, framing offers a way to describe the communicative power of a text. As set out by Entman (1993), framing involves selection and salience. To frame is to select aspects of a perceived reality and make them salient in a text, 'in such a way as to promote a particular problem definition, causal interpretation, moral evaluation, and/or treatment recognition for the item described' (Entman 1995, 5). By extension, Entman's framing paradigm directs attention to the ways in which the text exerts that power. For this reason, the authors of this article believe that framing is the best schema by which to examine the underlying power dynamics in news coverage of technology's role in the Egyptian revolution.

The frame in a news text can be considered the imprint of power, as it registers the identity of interests or actors that compete to dominate the text (Entman 1993, 55). Gamson (1992) argues that frames encoded in a particular terminology or touchstone idea (his example is 'affirmative action') exert particular social power once they are widely adopted. At that point, the employment of another frame risks having the target audience perceive the communicator as lacking credibility (Entman 1993, 55). One of the research goals here is to examine whether relevant terms such as 'Revolution 2.0' and 'Internet freedom', or ideas about protesters' reliance on social media and the repressive response of Mubarak's government, have become similarly indispensable to both Arab and Western mediated discourse.

In short, frames define problems, make moral judgements and suggest remedies. Framing is particularly useful for content analysis, as the paradigm can measure not only positive and negative terms, but also the salience of textual elements (Entman 1993, 52). Mindful of the news media's function as the primary dialogic forum for rapidly developing events, as well as its ability to shape the issue agendas of both the public and policymakers (e.g. McCombs and Shaw 1972), the focus therefore falls on the frames disseminated by media sources.

Research design

This article reports the results of a systematic content analysis of news articles, undertaken to explore how news sources from the West and the Arab/Middle East region framed the use of information and communications technology in the Egyptian revolution. The research questions were as follows:

RQ1: How did media sources describe technology use in relation to the Egyptian uprisings? Which technologies or tools were mentioned most frequently, and what role(s) were they reported to play in the revolution?

RQ2: How did media sources frame new technologies' potential use as an enabling tool for protest?

RQ3: How did media sources frame new technologies' potential use as repressive tools for authoritarian regimes?

RQ4: Did Western and Arab/Middle East region media sources employ consistently different frames on the use of technology in the Egyptian revolution, and its enabling or repressive potential?

Following Carragee and Roefs (2004, 217), it is evident that RQ1 investigates story topics (particular technologies) rather than frames. It has been included for descriptive purposes as well as for the potential comparison with research on the relative prevalence of various technologies among survey respondents, in Cairo, during the protests (Wilson and Dunn 2011). RQ2 and RQ3 take up the media/policy conversation on ICTs and democratisation, while RQ4 asks whether particular frames are predominant in Western or Arab/Middle East region news sources.

Method

Content analysis of print and online news media sources

The data derive from six major Western news sources – *The New York Times*, *Financial Times*, *The Wall Street Journal*, *USA Today*, *The Washington Post* and *The Times* of London – and six English-language Arab/Middle East region news sources: *Al-Sharq al-Awsat*, AlArabiya.net, Aljazeera.net, *The Daily Star* (Lebanon), *The Jerusalem Post* and *Tehran Times*. In both groups, the researchers aimed to select sources with some diversity in terms of political leaning and target audience, in addition to the practical consideration of sources being available in searchable English-language archives. The search criteria were as follows:

- Article contains 'Egypt', AND
- Article contains one of: 'protest', 'democracy', 'mobilisation', 'change', 'democratisation', 'revolution', AND
- Article contains one of: 'technology', 'new media', 'social media', 'social networking', 'Internet', 'website', 'Facebook', 'Twitter', 'SMS', 'text message', 'mobile phone'.

With the exception of Aljazeera.net, articles were obtained through institutional subscriptions to the news archive services Academic OneFile and Newsbank. For Aljazeera.net, the website's built-in search function was used to access articles directly.

The initial search yielded 583 articles. Of these, 388 were deemed relevant to the subject of the study, with the remainder being discarded because although they contained the search terms, they were not applied in the context of the use of technology during protests in the Arab world. Table 1 shows a breakdown of relevant article counts by source.

Table 1: Articles included in analysis, by source

Arab/Middle East region sources	Al-Sharq al-Awsat	11
	AlArabiya.net	33
	Aljazeera.net	10
	The Daily Star (Lebanon)	27
	The Jerusalem Post	30
	Tehran Times	15
Western sources	*Financial Times*	32
	The New York Times	75
	The Times of London	47
	USA Today	21
	The Wall Street Journal	29
	The Washington Post	58
	TOTAL	**388**

The content-analytic software Dedoose (www.dedoose.com) was chosen for the analysis. Coding was done by two independent coders, based on the codebook (Appendix A). Inter-coder reliability was assessed on a sample of 50 articles, achieving a Cohen's Kappa of .91. Coders were presented with the article title, date and text, but no information on the source,[2] and were asked to excerpt and code paragraph-length portions of text that mentioned technology in relation to the revolution. Coders were also asked to flag particularly dense articles that had technology as a major theme, with a view to examining these more closely as potential frame sources.

On completion of the coding, the resulting excerpts and codes were exported to a relational database to perform an aggregation step. Codes applied to one or more excerpts within a document were considered to be applied, at most once, to the document itself. The resulting dataset represents a document-level coding.

Statistical analyses were performed using SPSS. In addition to codes applied to each document, two dichotomous variables were created to represent the presence or absence of the two frames most commonly noted by coders: Frame 1, for articles that mentioned Facebook or Twitter in conjunction with positive uses of technology by protesters, and Frame 2 for articles that mentioned the Internet, mobile phones or text messaging in conjunction with repressive uses of technology by government (overwhelmingly the government-ordered shutdown of mobile networks and Internet service providers). A scale variable for the importance of technology to the revolution was created from the categories applied as codes (no bearing in the revolution=0, just one of many factors in the revolution=1, important in the revolution=2, indispensable in the revolution=3, the main factor in the revolution=4), and for convenience, additional dichotomous variables were created to identify articles from Arab/Middle East region sources, and articles that mentioned positive uses of technology by protesters or repressive uses of technology by government. These variables are shown in Table 2.

Table 2: Variables included in analysis

Variable	Metric	Distribution	Valid cases
Source from the Arab/Middle East region	no=0, yes=1	no=68%, yes=32%	388
Importance of technology in the revolution	no bearing=0, just one of many factors=1, important=2, indispensable=3, the main factor=4	no bearing=3%, just one of many factors=6%, important=41%, indispensable=40%, the main factor=10%	189
Frame 1 (Facebook or Twitter + positive use of tech by protesters)	absent=0, present=1	absent=59%, present=41%	388
Frame 2 (Internet, mobile phones or text messaging + repressive use of tech by government)	absent=0, present=1	absent=69%, present=31%	388

Results

RQ1: Describing technology use

As shown in Figure 1, about half the articles included implicit or explicit statements about the importance of technology to the revolution. For those that did, the distribution was approximately normal.

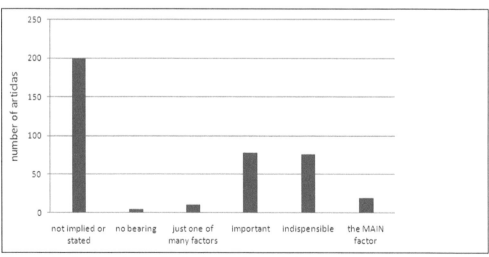

Figure 1: Implied importance of technology to the revolution

Descriptive statistics for mentions of particular technologies are shown in Table 3. For comparison, Figure 2 shows the percentages of articles mentioning Facebook, Twitter, mobile phones, text messaging and blogs, alongside data from Wilson and Dunn (2011) on the reported use of technology by respondents in Cairo, both in general and during the protests.

Table 3: Percentages of articles mentioning particular technologies

	% of articles
Internet (unspecified)	51%
Facebook	46%
Twitter	29%
Mobile phones	19%
Blogs or bloggers	9%
Social media (unspecified)	9%
Text messages/SMS	6%
YouTube	5%
Email	3%
Landline phones	3%
Web 1.0 (non-interactive)	2%
'New media' or 'new technology' (unspecified)	2%
Web 2.0 (unspecified)	1%
Visual media	1%
Flickr	0%

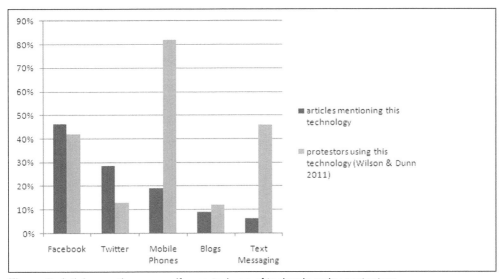

Figure 2: Article mentions vs. self-reported use of technology by protesters

It is not unexpected to find that the media covered certain technologies disproportionately to their use. For one thing, coverage is linked to events, and events such as Wael Ghonim's creation of the 'We are all Khaled Said' Facebook group, his subsequent arrest and pronouncements on Twitter, were significant. Mentions of Twitter in articles that mentioned Facebook were common – the conditional probability of articles that mentioned Facebook also mentioning Twitter was 73 per cent, while the reverse (conditional probability of articles that mentioned Twitter also mentioning Facebook) was only 29 per cent. Wilson and Dunn (2011) note further that despite the low use figures for Twitter, it proved an important channel for both the regional and the transnational dissemination of information. Media sources are ideally positioned to take up such information.

Revealingly, however, the extensive instrumental use of mobile phones and text messaging documented by Wilson and Dunn (2011) went largely unreported. Where mobile phones were mentioned, the context was largely related to the shutdown of mobile networks by government, rather than specific instrumental use by protesters (this was the case in 63 per cent of articles mentioning mobile phones).

RQ2: Framing technology as an enabler for protest

Fifty-eight percent (N=266) of the articles in the dataset were coded as implicitly or explicitly identifying the use of technology as an enabler for protest. A breakdown of coded uses by category is shown in Table 4.

For analysis, the set of uses in Table 4 was collapsed into the dichotomous variable 'positive uses of technology by protesters'. An independent samples t-test confirmed that the mean for this variable was not significantly different for Arab and Western sources. There was, however, a significant positive correlation between positive uses of technology by protesters and mentions of Twitter or Facebook ($r = .412$, $p < .001$), and a significant negative correlation ($r = -.251$, $p < .001$) with the Internet, text messaging or mobile phones. On this basis, the dichotomous variable 'Frame 1' was computed as true for articles mentioning Twitter or Facebook in conjunction with positive uses of technology by protesters.

Table 4: Technology use by protesters

Technology helped protesters to ...	% of articles
Organise on the ground	35%
Disseminate information about grievances	32%
Spark more protests in Egypt	12%
Spread protest to other countries	12%
Gain foreign media coverage	7%
Disseminate visual material (photos and video)	7%
Gain domestic media coverage	2%
Mobilise support from foreign governments	0%

RQ3: Framing technology as a tool for repression by government

Thirty-eight per cent (N=149) of the articles in the dataset were coded as implicitly or explicitly identifying the repressive use of technology by the Egyptian government, in an attempt to suppress protest. A breakdown of coded uses by category is shown in Table 5.

Table 5: Technology use by government

	% of articles
Internet, mobile networks or specific sites cut off – protesters' communication cut off	33%
Government can monitor protesters	5%
Low Internet penetration/low use of specific technologies	3%
Operators forced to send pro-Mubarak messages	1%
Fake statements disseminated	0%

As with RQ2, the categories in Table 5 were collapsed into a single dichotomous variable, 'repressive uses of technology by government'. An independent samples t-test confirmed no significant difference between Arab/Middle East region and Western sources in terms of the presence of this variable. There was a significant positive correlation between repressive uses of technology by government and mentions of Internet, mobile phones or text messaging ($r = .395$, $p < .001$), and a significant negative correlation of this variable with Twitter or Facebook ($r = -.269$, $p < .001$). On this basis, the dichotomous variable 'Frame 2' was computed as true for articles mentioning the Internet, mobile phones or text messaging in conjunction with repressive uses of technology by government.

RQ4: Differential framing by Western and Arab/Middle East region media

Articles in Western sources (N=262) did not mention Twitter or Facebook significantly more frequently than articles in Arab/Middle East region sources (N=126), nor were they significantly more likely to mention the positive or repressive use of technology, or to employ Frame 1 or Frame 2. This is visually confirmed in Figure 3.

An independent samples t-test comparing mean values for the reported importance of technology to the revolution showed a significantly lower mean for Arab/Middle East region sources (M=2.15, SD=1.01) than for Western sources (M=2.61, SD=.76), t(187)=3.34, p< .01. A linear regression controlling for the presence of Frame 1 or Frame 2 confirmed the significance and relative magnitude of this effect.

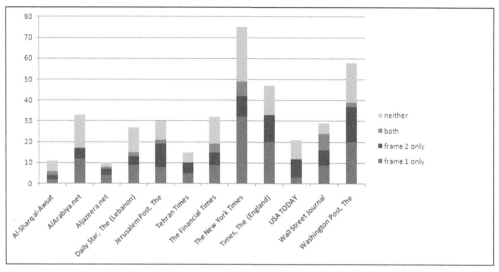

Figure 3: Frames employed by source

The *New York Times'* social media problem?

Working from an observation made during preliminary data analysis in Dedoose, the researchers examined article counts by source for articles that mentioned Twitter or Facebook and those that did not. The results, in Figure 4, suggest that the *New York Times* and *USA Today* might be anomalous in this regard. This was confirmed with a logistic regression (DV=mentions Twitter or Facebook, IV=*New York Times*, *USA Today*). On average, the *New York Times* was significantly more likely (p< .05) to mention Twitter or Facebook than other sources (excluding *USA Today*), while *USA Today* was significantly less likely (p< .01) to do so.

Discussion

Although differing in their implications of importance, Western and Arab/Middle East region news sources told a similar story about the role of technology in the Egyptian revolution. The story itself is coherent in its representation of technology both as an enabler for protest and as a tool for repression by the Egyptian government.

The specific technologies mentioned in news articles do not correspond directly to use on the ground. One explanation for this is that particular technologies – Facebook and Twitter – were seen as decisive or novel, while others, such as mobile phones, were not. The *New York Times* jubilantly headlined one article 'Tweets vs. Tanks in Tahrir', while Wael Ghonim was 'the Facebook dreamer who led his nation' in the *Times of London*.

For distant observers, social media use by Egyptians also offered a remarkably accessible first-hand account of events. Stories such as Wael Ghonim's arrest and Mohamed ElBaradei's return to Egypt were bolstered by tweeted quotes from the subjects themselves, and the high proportion of tweets in English (96% of all tweets with the hashtag #jan25 according to Wilson and Dunn [2011]) provided journalists with a ready stream of updates. In addition, 140-character tweeted jokes – 'uninstalling dictator, 99% complete!' – fed a triumphant story that captivated the West and the Arab world.

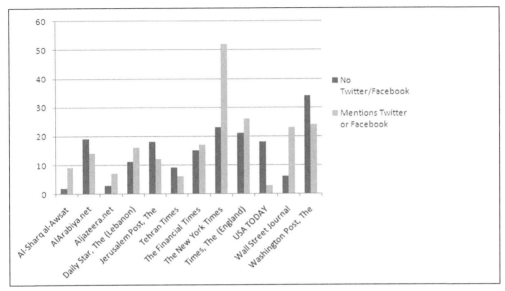

Figure 4: Mentions of Twitter or Facebook by source

The predominant frame on technology as an enabler for protest was similarly preoccupied with Facebook and Twitter as triumphant over other social media services and over other technologies generally. The instrumental use of social media to organise on the ground is belied by low penetration rates and the resilience of the demonstrations in the face of the Internet (and mobile network) shutdown.

The claim that social media were used to disseminate information about grievances is more interesting, but it should be noted that the international community was likely at least as much a target for dissemination efforts as ordinary Egyptians. By reporting the use of social media without this dimension, the news media promote a clearly delineated national sovereignty over more accurately blurred lines of the national and international. Facebook and Twitter are not impartial international institutions but US-based companies, and one assumes that the democratic value of 'Internet freedom' extends only as far as their interests are not threatened.

Beyond sparse mention of the above US policy, an analysis of the role of technology in statecraft is barely discernible in the media reports considered. Reporting on the repressive use of technology by the Egyptian government was confined almost entirely to mentions of the government-ordered shutdown of the Internet and, periodically, of mobile networks. The Egyptian government is portrayed as panicked and cowardly, prepared to shut off vital infrastructure and cripple the economy in a bid to suppress peaceful protest. Far less visible are the multinational companies that control the mobile networks and rely on the government for the right to operate in Egypt's lucrative mobile market. Under pressure, Vodaphone admitted to sending pro-Mubarak text messages to subscribers on their network, but the incident was barely reported. In the examined articles, surveillance of protesters – widely alleged in activist communities – leaves fewer traces still, and the instrumental, infrastructural portrayal of technology as a vital democratic institution is unchallenged.

Conclusion

It is somewhat surprising that this study revealed few differences between the Western and Middle East region news outlets in their framing of technology in the Egyptian protests. But this is very possibly due to the study's major limitation: the Middle East and Arab press outlets examined were all English-language publications or websites. These sources are written and edited, in part, for an international audience; a few even base their editorial offices in London. Further research of Arabic-language news outlets is needed to confirm whether similar systematic biases in covering the protests were to be found across mainstream media outlets internationally, or whether they differed significantly according to their regional target audience – an issue thoroughly imbued with the power dynamics inherent to 'democratisation'.

Indeed, while the policy implications of the framing of technology in the Egyptian revolution remain to be seen, the media reports examined are remarkably consistent with the US promotion of Internet freedom. As a tool for democratisation, technology is framed as novel and modern, neutral and unbeholden to corporate interests. Provided there is no overt evidence to the contrary, it is also expected that technology will operate without government interference. When interference is reported, it is portrayed as unsophisticated and probably ineffectual.

The effect of all this, much as in Curran's (2000) critique of the 'marketplace of ideas', is to render invisible persistent access and representation differentials on social media platforms, and in technology generally. Policy support for technology companies is legitimated in light of their provision of the infrastructure for democratisation. This is likely exacerbated by findings (by Loudon and Mazumdar) that indicate the high proportions of mentions given by the *New York Times* – the journalistic standard-bearer – to the very American companies of Facebook and Twitter in its coverage. At the same time, government surveillance, though ever-present, has disappeared amidst the clamour of a 'developing' public given voice.

Acknowledgements

The authors would like to thank Jeremy Salazar for research assistance with this project, as well as Patricia Riley, Yu Hong and Renyi Hong for comments on drafts of the manuscript.

Notes

1   Before the Mubarak government shut down Facebook in Egypt, Ghonim and others created the Facebook page called 'We are all Khaled Said,' dedicated to the memory of an Egyptian who,

witnesses maintain, was beaten to death in Alexandria by police officers who had not been held to account (Olivarez-Giles 2011).

2   While it was possible for coders to obtain this information from Dedoose, it was a time-consuming extra step and was discouraged.

References

ABC News. 2011, February 1. Egypt in crisis: Largest protest yet. Abcnews.com. http://abcnews.go.com/GMA/video/egypt-crisis-largest-protest-yet-12809642 (accessed 1 February 2011).

Avgerou, C. 2003. The link between ICT and economic growth in the discourse of development. In *Organizational information systems in the context of globalization*, ed. A. Poulymenakou, M. Korpela and R. Montealegre, 373–386. Athens: Springer. http://libeprints.lse.ac.uk/2575/1/The_link_between_ICT_and_economic_growth_in_the_discourse_of_development_(LSERO).pdf

Bennett, W.L. 2003. Communicating global activism: Strengths and vulnerabilities of networked politics. *Information, Communication and Society* 6(2): 143–168.

Bimber, B. 2000. The study of information technology and civic engagement. *Political Communication* 17(4): 329.

Brecher, M. 1972. *The foreign policy system of Israel: Setting, images, process*. Don Mills, Ont.: Oxford University Press.

Brosius, H.B. and H.M. Kepplinger. 1990. The agenda-setting function of television news: Static and dynamic views. *Communication Research* 17: 183–211.

Canel, M.J., J.P. Llamas and F. Rey. 1996. The first level agenda-setting effect on location information: The 'most important' problems of the city of Pamplona. *Communicacion y Sociedad* 9: 17–38.

Carragee, K.M. and W. Roefs. 2004. The neglect of power in recent framing research. *Journal of Communication* 54(2): 214–233.

Castells, M., M. Fernandez-Ardevol, J.L. Qiu and A. Sey. 2007. *Mobile communication and society: A global perspective.* Cambridge, MA: MIT Press.

CBS News. 2011, February 13. Wael Ghonim and Egypt's new age revolution. cbsnews.com. http://www.cbsnews.com/stories/2011/02/13/60minutes (accessed 13 February 2011).

Cook, F.L., T.R. Tyler, E.G. Goetz, M.T. Gordon, D. Protess, D.R. Leff and H.L. Molotch. 1983. Media and agenda setting: Effects on the public, interest group leaders, policy makers and policy. *The Public Opinion Quarterly* 47(1): 16–35.

Curran, J. 2000. Rethinking media and democracy. In *Mass media and society*, ed. J. Curran and M. Gurevitch, 120–154. London: Edward Arnold.

Diani, M. 2000. Social movement networks, virtual and real. *Information, Communication and Society* 31(3): 386–401.

Entman, R.M. 1993. Framing: Toward clarification of a fractured paradigm. *Journal of Communication* 43(4): 51–58.

Feenberg, A. 2005. Critical theory of technology: An overview. *Tailoring Biotechnologies* 1(1): 47–64.

Gamson, W. 1992. *Talking politics*. New York: Cambridge University Press.

Ghannam, J. 2011. Social media in the Arab world: Leading up to the uprisings of 2011. Report to the Center for International Media Assistance. http://cima.ned.org/sites/default/files/CIMA-Arab_Social_Media-Report_2.pdf (accessed 29 April 2011).

Gilboa, E. 1998. Secret diplomacy in the television age. *Gazette* 60: 211–225.

Gilboa, E. 2005. The CNN effect: The search for a communication theory of international relations. *Political Communication* 22: 27–44.

Granqvist, M. 2005. Assessing ICT in development: A critical perspective. In *Media and glocal change: Rethinking communication for development*, ed. O. Hemer and T. Tufte, 285–296. Buenos Aires: CLACSO.

G8 Digital Opportunities Task Force. 2001. Digital opportunities for all: Meeting the challenge. Report of the Digital Opportunities Task Force, including a proposal for the Genoa Plan of Action. Genoa: DOT Force. http://www.g7.utoronto.ca/summit/2001genoa/dotforce1.html (accessed 15 May 2008).

Hashem, S. 2002. Bridging the digital divide in Egypt: Facing the challenges. UNCTAD E-Commerce First Expert Meeting, 10–12 July. http://r0.unctad.org/ecommerce/event_docs/estrategies/hashem.pdf (accessed 20 April 2012).

Hester, J.B. and R. Gibson. 2003. The economy and second-level agenda-setting: A time series analysis of economic news and public opinion about the economy. *Journalism and Mass Communication Quarterly* 80: 73–90.

Holbrook, R.A. and T.G. Hill. 2005. Agenda-setting and priming in prime-time televisions: Crime dramas as political cues. *Political Communication* 22: 277–295.

International Telecommunication Union (ITU). 2012. *ICT adoption and prospects in the Arab region.* Geneva, Switzerland: ITU.

Kallinikos, J. 2004. Farewell to constructivism: Technology and context-embedded action. In *The social study of information and communication technology: Innovation, actors, and contexts*, ed. C. Avgerou, C. Ciborra and F. Land, 140–161. New York, NY: Oxford University Press.

Kamel, S. 2010. Information and communications technology for development: Building the knowledge society in Egypt. In *Access to knowledge in Egypt: New research on intellectual property, innovation and development*, ed. N. Rizk and L.B. Shaver, 174–204. London and New York: Bloomsbury Academic.

Kanalley, C. 2011, April 1. Egypt revolution 2011: A complete guide to the unrest. Huffingtonpost. com. http://www.huffingtonpost.com/2011/01/30/egypt-revolution-2011_n_816026.html (accessed 6 February 2013).

Klein, H.K. 1999. Tocqueville in cyberspace: Using the Internet for citizen associations. *The Information Society* 15(4): 213–220.

Lennon, F.R. 1998. *The 1997 Argentina election: The national dailies and the electoral campaign.* Report by the Freedom Forum and Austral University.

Lichtenstein, J. 2011, February 2. Did Twitter make them do it? Slate.com. http://www.slate.com/id/2283615 (accessed 2 February 2011).

Mahmud, T. 1999. Postcolonial imaginaries: Alternative development or alternatives to development? SSRN eLibrary. http://papers.ssrn.com.libproxy.usc.edu/sol3/papers.cfm?abstract_id=1433562 (accessed 11 March 2011).

McCombs, M. and A. Reynolds. 2009. How the news shapes our civic agenda. In *Media effects: Advances in theory and research*, 3rd edition, ed. J. Bryant and M.B. Oliver, 1–16. New York: Erlbaum.

McCombs, M. and D. Shaw. 1972. The agenda-setting function of mass media. *Public Opinion Quarterly* 36: 176–187.

Moodley, S. 2005. The promise of e-development? A critical assessment of the state ICT for poverty reduction discourse in South Africa. *Perspectives on Global Development and Technology* 4(1): 1–26.

MSNBC. 2011, January 31. The Rachel Maddow Show, Friday, 28 January. Msnbc.com. http://www.msnbc.msn.com/id/41351005/ns/msnbc_tv-rachel_maddow_show/ (accessed 31 January 2011).

Naveh, C. 2002. The role of the media in foreign policy decision-making. *Conflict and Communication Online* 1(2): 1–14.

Neuendorf, K.A. 2002. *The content analysis guidebook*. Thousand Oaks, CA: Sage Publications, Inc.

Peter, J. 2003. Country characteristics as contingent conditions as agenda setting: The moderating influence of polarized elite opinion. *Communication Research* 30: 683–712.

Rheingold, H. 2002. *Smart mobs: The next social revolution*. New York: Perseus Books Group.

Rich, F. 2011, February 5. Wallflowers at the revolution. *The New York Times*. http://www.nytimes.com (accessed 5 February 2011).

Schech, S. 2002. Wired for change: The links between ICTs and development discourses. *Journal of International Development* 14(1): 13–23.

Shirky, C. 2011. The political power of social media. Foreign Affairs. http://www.foreignaffairs.com/articles/67038/clay-shirky/the-political-power-of-social-media (accessed 27 April 2011).

Stahl, B. 2008. Empowerment through ICT: A critical discourse analysis of the Egyptian ICT policy. In *Social dimensions of information and communication technology policy*, ed. C. Avgerou, M.L. Smith and P. van den Besselaar, 161–177. New York: Springer.

Summers, P. 2011, March 3. McCain: Zuckerberg made Middle East revolutions possible. Foxnews.com. http://politics.blogs.foxnews.com/2011/03/03/mccain-zuckerberg-made-middle-east-revolutions-possible (accessed 3 March 2011).

Thompson, M. 2004. Discourse, 'development' and the 'digital divide': ICT and the World Bank. *Review of African Political Economy* 31(99): 103–123.

Tilly, C. 2003. Social movements enter the twenty-first century. University of Crete, Rethimno. http://falcon.arts.cornell.edu/sgt2/PSCP/documents/tilly2003-03.pdf (accessed 15 May 2008).

Warschauer, M. 2003. Dissecting the 'digital divide': A case study in Egypt. *The Information Society* 19(4): 297–304.

Wilson, C. and A. Dunn. 2011. Digital media in the Egyptian revolution: Descriptive analysis from the Tahrir data sets. *International Journal of Communication* 5: 1248–1272.

Winter, J.P. and C.H. Eyal. 1981. Agenda-setting for the civil rights issue. *Public Opinion Quarterly* 45: 376–383.

Wray, S. 1999. On electronic civil disobedience. *Peace Review* 11(1): 107–111.

A forgotten tweet: Somalia and social media

Skye Cooley and Amy Jones

Abstract

Several studies highlight the power of social media outlets to raise awareness, funds, and further recovery efforts in disaster-prone areas, but few have investigated where social media have been ineffectual. Although the long-running humanitarian crisis in Somalia receives only sporadic news coverage, the country is not without a social media presence. This study uses Coombs' SCCT Model to evaluate the crisis response message strategies put forth via Twitter from leading Somali-based government agency sources. The limitations of social media as a force to exact change and manage crises in Africa is examined, and insight is offered into how social media channel information to traditional and non-traditional information sources.

Introduction

The purpose of this study is to evaluate the crisis response message strategies, put forth via social media by leading Somali-based government agency sources, using a modified version of Coombs' Situational Crisis Communication Theory (SCCT) Model (Coombs 2004). This study aims to help scholars better understand the usage of social media in Africa in respect of disaster relief, how social media offer the ability to link users to traditional and non-traditional information sources, and what the limitations may be of the social media as exactors of change.

Several studies have shown the power of social media to aid otherwise disenfranchised and impoverished citizens in political organisation, protest and revolution (Beaubien 2011; Jacques 2011). Others have pointed out the power of social media outlets to raise awareness and funds, and aid further recovery efforts in areas impacted by disaster (Crowe 2011; McCafferty 2011; Simmons 2010). Few studies have, however, investigated those instances where the social media have been ineffective in rallying support, increasing aid, and/or rallying the masses to protest and revolution. One of the lengthiest and most devastating humanitarian crises in recent years has been that of

Somalia. And while the country has received sporadic news coverage, it has not been without a social media presence. This study will detail how social media messages are being delivered in a manner that, compared to other similar, scaled disasters, has been ineffectual. It will also allow for comparisons that will better our understanding of what role social media message strategy has in motivating traditional media and the masses in response.

The analysis of this research starts at the beginning of June 2011, when Doctors Without Borders (2011) reported an emerging humanitarian emergency due to overcrowding from Somalis fleeing an increasingly severe famine and drought. It concludes at the end of September 2011, and the start of the October rainy season, at which point the United Nations (UN) Office for the Coordination of Humanitarian Affairs' (OCHA 27 September 2011) report claimed that nearly 1.5 million people were internally displaced, 917 000 had refugee status, and a total of four million Somalis were in crisis as a result of the summer drought.

Review of the literature

The Somali famine crisis

This research attempts to explore the connections between the famine crisis in Somalia, and the use of social media to encourage donations and spread awareness of the crisis. To understand how the social media can be used in a time of crisis, one needs to know the background of the catastrophe, and how traditional and social media have been used in similar situations.

On 20 July 2011, the UN officially declared a famine in Somalia (Warah 2011). By the end of that month, more than 29 000 children in that country had died of hunger, and this had been declared the worst Somali famine crisis in over 60 years (Griswold 2011). Warah (2011) explains that famine is officially declared when malnutrition among children reaches 30 per cent, among other criteria. Experts on the topic blamed the famine on an intense drought, but also attributed some of the food shortages to political unrest in the region (Ball and Rice 2011; Griswold 2011). With no forecasts being made for rain in the region, it was argued that the death toll could surpass one million people, with another estimate of ten million being affected by food shortages (Ball and Rice 2011). Ball and Rice argue that these numbers qualify the Somali famine to be declared five times worse than other recent notable disasters and crises, such as the earthquake in Haiti and the tsunami in Asia. However, in comparison the Somali crisis has received far less media coverage, and very little relief funding.

Ball and Rice (2011) estimate that the crisis in Somalia has received less than half of the attention and aid of recent disasters. Still, the UN estimated that US$2.5 million was needed for the humanitarian response in Somalia, yet there is a shortage of journalists on the ground to report those needs worldwide. Clearly, the media are a vital tool in expressing this need to the world. Yet, the very nature of a famine in an unsecured nation is a difficult situation for journalists to conquer using traditional media outlets. In a crisis such as the one in Somalia, social media networks arguably provide a media voice to people living in those areas, and also to organisations trying to secure aid (such as the UN). It is therefore important to understand how relief organisations and others use social media outlets in times of crisis.

Social media and Twitter

Social networking sites have changed the way organisations and businesses communicate with the public. This communication is instant, inexpensive, worldwide and targeted (Christ 2005). In other words, it differs from more traditional media outlets. Multiple social networks have been developed, each with their own distinct features. These social networks include MySpace, Facebook, Twitter and LinkedIn. For the purpose of analysing the social media messages sent by the UN and the African Union (AU), this research analysed tweeted messages, which necessitates further explanation of the use of Twitter.

Twitter and tweeting: Twitter became widely popular in 2007 after being launched just one year earlier. It allows users to post messages (of 140 characters or fewer) to a rapidly growing, targeted audience (an established group of followers). In 2010 there were more than 100 million users, with an estimated addition of 135 000 new users each day. Posts by Twitter users are commonly known as 'tweets'. It is estimated that there are more than two billion tweets per month (Sutter 2010). Twitter enables individuals to seek information (posted in tweets) via two methods: exposure will occur if an individual is a follower of a specific page, or is a user of the keyword search. Therefore, creating content is a public way of disseminating information (Oreskovic 2010). Users can search for tweets containing content pertaining to the famine in Somalia, if desired. For this reason, Twitter was the social media network of choice for the present research. Because participation via tweets is social in nature, Twitter is classified as a social medium.

The many uses of social media networks: Social media sites have become much more than a means of socialising with friends and colleagues. A body of research suggests that social media sites are gaining numerous uses, including spreading news worldwide about crises and revolution (Comunello and Anzera 2012; Joseph 2012). Savage (2011) argues that researchers and historians can use social media sites to examine culture and people's way of life. The data flows presented on these networks suggest an interest in sports, culture, politics and society. They can warn of natural disasters, the spread of disease, and even spread the use of slang, writing styles and stereotypes prevalent at the time (Savage 2011).

These very foundations of social media networks are evident in the United States, as researchers argue that they help promote democracy. Samuels (2011) states that protests at the University of California in 2009 were hard to predict and control, because protesters turned to social media to form spontaneous groups of protestors. There are no gatekeepers in social media, and they have truly become the media sources of the people. Word can spread quickly and can influence the behaviours and actions of others (ibid.). Social media sites can enable voters, journalists and politicians to freely communicate with one another (Edna 2011).

Research indicates that social media networks are also useful for nations in distress, and in times of crisis. In emerging countries, government control of traditional media outlets has highlighted the desperate need for open communication among citizens (Smith 1995). The UN is helpful in developing media outlets in these areas, and social media outlets have proved to be the least restricted. Finally, government agencies have used social media sites to communicate quickly to mass audiences. Tucker (2011) argues that social media sites are used to send alerts much more quickly than traditional media outlets.

Challenges of traditional media coverage in times of crisis

Research indicates that traditional media sources encounter numerous challenges in times of crisis. Here, traditional media outlets have a different feel from social media outlets. Research suggests that traditional media outlets no longer carry the same level of public trust. Jurisic, Kanizaj, Jokos, Janez and Juric (2007) found that national media sources in underdeveloped nations frequently use media messages to trick the public. They observed that newspaper advertisements were frequently disguised to appear as newspaper articles. This event, and others, have led to traditional media outlets being distrusted in many developing countries (Jurisic et al. 2007).

Other researchers argue that releasing messages via traditional media outlets is tricky in regards to timing and frequency. Traditional media outlets not only cost more money for the time and/or space used, but the time and money required to produce a video, commercial or article are also enhanced. Therefore, a lag develops between the event itself and information being released to the public. If the information is released via news programming, the release can interrupt regular programming. Furthermore, the information is likely to be released with little frequency over a short period of time. Research suggests that this can backfire (Wei et al. 2010).

Despite the known disadvantages, traditional media outlets are still used by the UN during times of crisis management. The UN is known for its quick media response to crises, it uses the media to distance itself from any scandal, and it takes the opportunity to spread specific messages to the public (Capelos and Wurzer 2009). This suggests that traditional media outlets are not necessarily out of date; rather they have a different purpose than social media outlets.

Reporters Without Borders (8 May 2011) argues that in many crises situations, it is not safe to harbour journalists or traditional media outlets in affected areas, since 'local journalists work in terrible security conditions, caught in the crossfire from the fighting, and are often deliberately targeted by anti-media militiamen'. In these situations, social media become the primary means for disseminating information to the public.

The need for social media in developing countries is evident. Smith (1995) argues that such sources are often controlled by government agencies. Access to social media enables news and messages about the level of need to spread more quickly and safely. Therefore, an analysis of the social media messages disseminated during the famine crisis in Somalia is needed.

Crisis communication and the Situational Crisis Communication Theory (SCCT) model

This research utilised Coombs' (2006) SCCT as a guide to explore the communication strategies needed in times of crisis. It is important to understand that there are different types of crisis, and research indicates that the response strategies used should be appropriate to the situation. Fearn-Banks (1996, 1) defines a crisis as 'a major occurrence with a potentially negative outcome affecting an organization, company, or industry, as well as its publics, products, services, or good name'. Furthermore, research has attempted to typecast crises into various categories, including: economic, informational, physical, human resources, reputational, psycho-pathetic acts and natural disasters (Mitroff 2005). Here, the types of crisis are organised into groups based on the issue of origin.

Research suggests that while researchers divide crises into seven categories, organisations tend to use only two: the cobra and the python (Ahmed 2006). A cobra crisis is one that strikes suddenly, without warning. This type of crisis is unexpected, and frequently ends reasonably quickly. A python crisis is slower to unfold; it may involve numerous strikes, and often develops on multiple smaller issues.

The body of research on crisis communication is evidence that the SCCT is one of the most widely used models in this area. Coombs' (2006) theory tackles the research on crisis communication in three steps: the situation, the response strategies, and the development of a system that matches the two. Coombs identifies different types of crises, and the famine in Somalia (because it resulted from a natural disaster) can be classified in the 'victims' cluster, where even the UN, journalists and countries that come to the aid of Somali refugees, can be considered victims (ibid.).

In terms of response strategies (including social media messages), Coombs (ibid.) argues that organisations need to keep the focus on the victims, to reduce negative affect, and to prevent the formation of a poor reputation. Research indicates that response strategies which focus on the victims, are most effective (Coombs and Holladay 2004). Coombs' SCCT model identifies ten crisis communication strategies from three response clusters:

- Deny response cluster (Attack strategies – involving a confrontation, Denial strategies – denial that the crisis exists, Scapegoat strategies – blame the crisis on another entity);

- Diminish response cluster (Excuse strategies – make excuses for the organisation, and Justification strategies – minimise the damage and rationalise decisions/ actions); and

- Deal response cluster (Ingratiation strategies – praise stakeholders for good work, Concern strategies – repeatedly express concern for victims, Compassion strategies – offer money and other gifts to victims, Regret strategies – organisation feels bad about the crisis, and Apology strategies – organisation takes full responsibility for the crisis).

Finally, the foundation of the SCCT model suggests that care must be taken to match the crisis with the appropriate response strategy (Coombs 2006). In other words, an organisation can minimise negative affect by selecting the response strategy most appropriate to the type of crisis.

The purpose of this research is to analyse the response strategies used by the aid organisations in the Somali famine crisis – a victims-clustered crisis. As previously mentioned, this crisis was unique in that response tactics employing traditional media outlets were limited. Therefore, this research will analyse the response strategies put forth using social media.

RQ1: What response strategies were utilised by the UNHCRSomalia and AMISOM Twitter accounts following the July 2011 declaration of famine in two regions of southern Somalia?

RQ2: What was the most frequently used crisis communication strategy from the SCCT?

RQ3: Did the UNHCRSomalia and AMISOM Twitter accounts differ in message strategy?

RQ4a: What was the most frequently directed source for the UNHCRSomalia Twitter account?

RQ4b: What was the most frequently directed source for the AMISOM Twitter account?

RQ5a: How often were refugees themselves specifically quoted within the messages?

RQ5b: Did the UNHCRSomalia and AMISOM Twitter accounts differ in amount of usage of direct quotes and interviews of refugees?

RQ6: What were the most dominant relief effort concerns mentioned?

Method

To answer the research questions, the researchers conducted a content analysis. Budd, Thorp and Donohew (1967) describe content analysis as a systematic technique for analysing message content and message handling, whereby the analyst is not necessarily concerned with the message, but with the larger questions of the processes of effects and communication. For this case study, content analysis allows for an examination of all corporate crisis communication messages via Twitter to the public, through the lens of the SCCT model.

Implementing Coombs' crisis response strategies clusters, the researchers constructed a coding sheet to guide content analysis. The researchers chose to code all available publicly released tweets from @UNHCRSomalia and @AMISOM Twitter accounts from the beginning of June until September (this was when Doctors Without Borders reported an emerging humanitarian emergency due to overcrowding from Somalis fleeing an increasing famine and drought), as well as the linked sites (if present) from each Twitter post. This was done to determine, in totality, how the two largest (in terms of followers) English-language Twitter accounts officially endorsed and completely focused on the nation of Somalia, in presenting the drought and famine crisis during Summer 2011 in the Horn of Africa. @UNHCRSomalia, which has a Twitter following of over 4 000, is the official Twitter account of UNHCRSomalia. The goal of the United Nations High Commissioner for Refugees (UNHCR) is to lead and coordinate international efforts to protect refugees. The audience of the UNHCR are those with a 'singular determination to help the world's displaced and to help raise awareness about the suffering and needs of the vulnerable' (UNHCR 2012). @AMISOM, which boasts over 5 000 Twitter followers, is the official account of the African Union Mission to Somalia. AMISOM's mandate is to support dialogue, reconciliation and disarmament, to offer humanitarian assistance and monitor volatile areas. AMISOM's audience includes all supporters of stakeholders working towards stability in Somalia (AMISOM 2012).

Coders recorded the message from each Twitter post, the source of any linked site, along with the message from that link (press release, press conference, interview, news story, official speech, etc.) and the date of the message. All Twitter communications from these accounts, from the first posting in June to the last posting in September, were coded.

The site sources used by the accounts to communicate to the public at large via Twitter were coded into the following four categories: news media outlets, social media sites (Facebook, blogs, YouTube, etc.), UN- and African government-managed sites. The direct speakers of each linked site source were coded into the following categories: UN officials and employees, officials and employees of non-Somali African government bodies, activists/volunteers, news media, officials and employees of the Somali government, and Somali refugees.

Coders analysed each message using the original ten crisis communication strategies from the three response clusters outlined in Coombs' model. The researchers opted to divide the original Justification strategy outlined in the Coombs model into two separate categories, within an expanded 'Diminish' cluster. The researchers added a category of Minimisation, defined as: an organisation minimising the perceived damage caused by the crisis, and they retained the category of Justification, defined as: rationalising of an organisation's actions. These alterations were made after intercoder tests revealed a clear division of two individual categories within the original Justification strategy. The researchers of this study feel the addition adds greater depth to analyses used in the current study.

For each outgoing message, coders recorded the number of responses within the message (rather than doing a simple 'present' or 'absent' analysis). Thus, each message was analysed for the type of response, as well as the frequency of that response within the message. Notably, some messages contained none of the identified categories. The number of recorded responses was summed for each individual cluster, creating three scales (Deny, Diminish and Deal).

Descriptive statistics and *t*-tests were used to analyse the data and answer the research questions posed.

Results

Research question 1 asked what response strategies were utilised by the UNHCRSomalia and AMISOM Twitter accounts following the July 2011 declaration of famine in two regions of southern Somalia.

UNHCRSomalia (n=119) and AMISOM (n=53) employed a total of 172 textual or video-linked tweets via Twitter, in dealing with the 2011 Somali drought and famine from 1 June, when Doctors Without Borders reported an emerging humanitarian emergency, through to the end of September and the start of the October rainy season.

Of the 172 tweets with textual or video-linked content, 390 were crisis response message strategies, which included Ingratiation (n=98, 25%), Concern (n=87, 22%), Scapegoat (n=52, 13%), Justification (n=42, 11%), Compassion (n=37, 9%), Excuse (n=36, 9%), Minimisation (n=24, 6%), Attack (n=6, 2%), Denial (n=4, 1%), Regret (n=3, 1%), and Apology (n=1, .2%). The dominance of the Ingratiation and Concern strategies reflects the importance sought in pointing out the good work of both organisations, and showing compassion for the suffering. However, the high usage of Scapegoat and Justification also allude to a desire to blame-shift and to rationalise the protracted nature of the crisis.

Research question 2 asked what the most frequently used crisis communication strategy from the SCCT was.

Of the total message strategies, the majority came from the Deal cluster (n=226, 57.9%), followed by Diminish (n=102, 26.1%) and Deny (n=62, 20%).

The UNHCRSomalia account featured 248 message strategies. The Deal cluster was used most often (n=134, 54%), followed by Diminish (n=69, 27.8%) and Deny (n=45, 18.2%). The most common individual message strategies were: Concern (n=59, 23.7%), Ingratiation (n=47, 18.9%), Scapegoat (n=36, 14.5%), Excuse (n=32, 12.9%), and Justification (n=30, 12%).

The AMISOM account featured 142 message strategies. The Deal cluster was used most often (n=92, 65%), followed by Diminish (n=33, 23%) and Deny (n=17, 12%). The most common individual message strategies were Ingratiation (n=51, 36%), Concern (n=28, 20%), Minimisation (n=17, 12%), Scapegoat (n=16, 11%) and Justification (n=12, 8%).

Both organisations used the Deal cluster most frequently in an attempt to address the crisis, rather than diminishing the crisis or denying that a crisis was taking place. For both organisations, the frequent use of the Deal cluster points to a belief that the crisis was manageable.

Research question 3 asked if the UNHCRSomalia and AMISOM Twitter accounts differ in terms of message strategy.

Cluster differences

A *t*-test was used to examine mean differences between the two Twitter accounts' use of message strategy clusters; significance was set at .05. The study found significant differences between the UNHCRSomalia (n=119, m=1.12, std= .08) and the AMISOM (n=53, m=1.73, std= .10) accounts in their use of the Deal cluster (t= 4.07, df=170, p < .05).

The higher percentage usage of the Deal cluster by AMISOM suggests that the organisation was more likely to present the crisis as manageable. AMISOM's higher presentation of the crisis as one to be dealt with, may indicate a greater desire to present the crisis as one that could be contained.

There were no significant differences between the Deny and Diminish clusters for the two accounts.

Individual strategy differences

T-tests were used to examine the mean differences in individual message strategy between the two Twitter accounts. In total, 11 t-tests were conducted. As a control for potential error inflation, the significance level was lowered to .01. For the two accounts, the study found three significant differences between individual strategy use:

- UNHCRSomalia (n=119, m=.05, std= .23) was significantly less likely to use the Minimisation strategy than AMISOM (n=53, m=.32, std= .47), (t=4.85, df=170, p < .01). Minimisation of the crisis by AMISOM was more frequent, potentially due to its role in maintaining peace in volatile areas. The lack of minimisation of the part of the UNHCR is logical, considering its fundraising abilities are likely better served when a crisis is magnified, rather than minimised;

- UNHCRSomalia (n=119, m= .39, std= .49) was significantly less likely to use the Ingratiation strategy than AMISOM (n=53, m=.96, std= .19), (t=8.12, df=170, p < .01). AMISOM displayed a clear desire to highlight the good work of their efforts. It is possible to speculate that the UNHCR would want to do the same; however, the AU and its peacekeeping forces have reported past and present problems of ineptitude in the UNHCR handling crises and political turmoil (Feldman 2008; McKaiser 2012). The constant expression of Ingratiation points to a potential desire to depict AMISOM as a capable, collective force in the face of a mounting crisis.

- UNHCRSomalia (n=119, m= .26, std= .44) was significantly more likely to use the Excuse strategy than AMISOM (n=53, m= .07, std= .26), (t=2.93, df=170, p < .01). While the mean scores in both cases are low, the significantly lower mean score for AMISOM is a possible reflection of the aforementioned desire to prove itself capable in the face of a crisis. With excuses and ineptitude being major criticisms leveled by the AU, it is logical to see why AMISOM avoided this strategy.

Research question 4a asked what the most frequently directed source for the UNHCRSomalia Twitter account was.

The UNHCRSomalia (n=119) account used a variety of sources, with the Twitter account (n=53, 44.5%) being used most frequently. The most frequent directed sources were the news media sites (n=29, 24.4%), UN-managed websites (n=26, 21.8%), the YouTube social media website (n=6, 5%) and, finally, African government-managed websites (n=5, 4.2%).

Research question 4b asked what the most frequently directed source for the AMISOM Twitter account was.

The AMISOM (n=53) account directed every single message away from the Twitter account, yet virtually all of them were to the African government-managed websites, specifically the AU site (n=49, 92.5%). The remainder (n=6, 5%) were all directed to the AU's YouTube channel.

The distinction between directing Twitter users to news sources (as in the case of UNHCRSomalia), and a self-contained site (as in the case of AMISOM), is potentially highly significant and is discussed in full below. Based on these findings it is possible to speculate on potential credibility issues surrounding AMISOM.

Research question 5a asked how often refugees themselves were specifically quoted within the messages.

Of a total of 172 tweets from both Twitter accounts, only 40 (23.2%) gave quotes and interviews from the refugees themselves.

Research question 5b asked if the UNHCRSomalia and AMISOM Twitter accounts differed in terms of the amount of usage of direct quotes and interviews with refugees.

A *t*-test was used to examine the mean differences between the two Twitter accounts in terms of amount of voice given to refugees; significance was set at .05. The UNHCRSomalia account (n=119, m=.30, std= .46) gave significantly more voice to refugees than did the AMISOM account (n=53, m=.07, std= .26), (t= 3.34, df=170, p < .05). The significantly lower mean score for AMISOM points to a potential difference in focus. While providing stories and quotes from suffering refugees might aid efforts at procuring donations for UNHCRSomalia, such efforts are possibly counter to AMISOM showing that it maintains stability and performs good deeds.

Research question 6 asked what dominant relief effort concerns were mentioned.

Of a total of 172 tweets, the most dominant relief effort concern related to the devastating humanitarian crisis, compounded by a lack of resources. In 66 (38%) tweets, the humanitarian crisis was mentioned as being compounded by a lack of resources. Children were mentioned as the main victims of the crisis in 55 (32%) tweets.

Only on very rare occasions were aid workers and those who made donations (n=14, 8%) thanked outright. On even fewer occasions was mention made of the refugee camps and the relief effort as providing a new life/opportunity for refugees (n=10, 5%).

Furthermore, AMISOM did not mention, on a single occasion, the refugee camps and relief effort as indicative of a new life/opportunity, nor were any aid workers thanked outright. And while the two Twitter accounts were similar in terms of the percentage presenting the humanitarian crisis as being compounded by a lack of resources (AMISOM n=18, 34%, UNHCRSomalia n=48, 40.3%), AMISOM had only five (9.4%) of its tweets mentioning children as the main victims of the crisis, whereas 50 (42%) of UNHCRSomalia's tweets did so.

Discussion

The aim of this research was to investigate how social media sites can be used in times of crisis resulting from a natural disaster, such as the famine in Somalia. The crisis response strategies were coded from two English-speaking Twitter accounts: the UN (UNHCRSomalia) and the AU (AMISOM). Both organisations were attempting to use Twitter to spread the word about the famine crisis, garner support and encourage aid from individuals, organisations and other countries around the world. Holistically, more than half of the coded tweets used the Deal cluster, as identified in the SCCT model (Coombs 2006). This finding potentially suggests that both entities (the UN and the AU) responded to the famine by dealing with the crisis, rather than denying or diminishing its severity. More specifically, the tweets praised stakeholders (such as UN and AU aid workers) and showed concern for the Somali victims and refugees.

Response strategies and the Somali famine

While both the UN and the AU tweets fell within the Deal cluster, significant differences were found between the response strategies of the two organisations. The UN was significantly more likely to use the Excuse strategy (articulating excuses for the cause of the crisis – lack of resources, a lack of funding, extreme drought), while the AU was more likely to use Ingratiation (focusing more on the deeds of AU soldiers and praising their efforts to mitigate the crisis) (ibid.). UNHCRSomalia tweets linked to sites claiming that '[r]elief operations have been constrained by the security situation in Somalia' (13 July 2011) and that 'rebels hinder food shipments and [we] struggle to fill shortfalls in funding to respond to the disaster, despite constant international appeals' (8 August 2011).

AMISOM tweet links often made statements such as 'I am sure that [we] would be remembered of having contributed to the peace process not only in Somalia but in our continent of Africa' (12 September 2011) and 'to support the Somali people with the little resources we have by sharing our drinking water as well as continue to providing medical assistance to the people' (3 August 2011).

This finding is interesting, as it suggests differences between the two organisations and their social media followers. Coombs (2002) argues that crisis responses shared via media networks reflect the organisation's feelings about the crisis itself. Given this line of thinking, the UN potentially viewed the crisis as preventable or repairable if enough relief aid were sent, while the AU's strategy suggested the crisis would have been much worse, were it not for the hard work and aid already received from donors, workers and volunteers. It is possible to speculate on the AU's need to show solidarity and resolve, and its efforts to ingratiate itself to a critical global community placed the onus on message strategies to reflect its capability.

Interestingly enough, the SCCT model separates different types of crises into three categories, namely minimal responsibility (crisis due to natural disaster), low responsibility (accidental crisis), and strong responsibility (preventable crisis) (Coombs 2007). The Somali crisis clearly falls into the first category, because it was a natural disaster, not caused by human error. Therefore, the SCCT model recommends that

Excuse and/or Justification strategies are the appropriate response (Coombs 2006). However, with the Somali famine crisis, both the UN and the AU employed response tactics that fall into the Deal cluster, which is more commonly used with a higher level of crisis responsibility. In other words, the tweets for both organisations suggest they blamed themselves and the Somalis for the disaster. More specifically, the UN appeared more willing to take the blame, while the AU largely appeared to blame the Somalis by focusing on praising their own efforts.

Citing sources in social media

Next, the results suggest another difference between the UN and the AU Twitter posts, in terms of how each cited sources for the information provided. The citation of sources on social media sites is vital in establishing a perception of credibility (Simmons 2010). Based on this assumption, the UN Twitter feed was perceived as more credible than that of the AU. Most of the UN Twitter posts cited other tweets, other traditional media sources and the websites of other relief organisations. Only 21 per cent of the tweets cited information coming from the UN itself. However, the AU mostly cited itself – a non-traditional information source – in the form of its own websites. More than 92 per cent of the AU tweets cited information coming from AU-controlled websites. Therefore, conceivably, the AU tweets were likely to be perceived as less credible than the UN tweets. It is vital to understand the use of non-traditional information source links and their impact on credibility. The AU, an institution fraught with credibility concerns (Feldman 2008), most likely did little to lessen that perception by using its own websites as linkages to further information.

Through these citations, both organisations show the reality of Somali victims and refugees. No effort was made to gloss over the gross reality of refugees' suffering. The refugee camps, described as being in a horrible condition, were often shown in photographs with appeals such as this UNHCRSomalia post: '[T]hese [pictures] from Somalia are just heartbreaking and make me ashamed to be human, [please] support' (28 July 2011). Still, differences found in the tweets arguably reflect the purpose of each organisation. The AU arguably minimised the negative reality of refugee camps more than the UN, as the AU is responsible for military operations in Mogadishu, and therefore tends to show appreciation for the work of soldiers there (The African Union Commission). The UN is responsible for attracting relief aid. Since less aid than expected was sent to curb the Somali crisis, it is only logical for them to exacerbate the deplorable living conditions of refugees. Here, they focused more on the lack of resources and infrastructure that curtailed the effectiveness of their organisation. Still, the UN did place greater focus on the Somali children who were victims, as 32 per cent of tweets focused on young children – again, such efforts are likely a way to appeal for more aid.

Conclusion

The famine in Somalia proved difficult for support and relief organisations, given the sheer scope of the crisis. The failure to raise adequate relief funding for such a monumental crisis is curious, given the ease of message distribution in a digitally connected world. Furthermore, since famine in Somalia is a recurring crisis (albeit every 60 years or so, to this degree of severity), the reaction of other government agencies, individuals and volunteers was arguably not as immediate and strong as in other recent and rare crises (e.g., the Asian tsunami). Further research on the role of such intensifiers might shed light on more appropriate message strategies for similar relief efforts in the future. Undoubtedly, the repeated failures of proper food supply to the Horn of Africa have made the image of the starving African common to Western audiences, perhaps thus impacting constraint recognition and limiting the ability of any media, without a radically different message approach, of succeeding in raising funds. These factors, and no doubt several potential others, led to an extreme shortage in aid to victims in the region. Relief organisations turned to social media outlets as a major means of distributing information to the public, yet even this new form of message delivery was seemingly inadequate.

This research highlights a growing use for social media – rather than a means of connecting with friends and networking, it is becoming increasingly used as a tool for aid agencies involved in relief efforts. Here, Twitter was regularly used to spread the word about the needs of Somali victims and refugees. Furthermore, the SCCT model was effective in highlighting how Twitter feeds from the UN and the AU collectively show that both organisations feel responsible for problems in reducing the scope of the crisis. Finally, this research sheds light on how different relief organisations use social media to promote their own organisation (through self-citations and links to non-traditional information sources) and agendas, even in times of crisis. It is the hope of this research team that identified failures in raising funds and awareness (in the case of Somalia) will lead to a refinement and improvement of message strategies in regions facing recurring crises, and will further our understanding of the power and limitations of the social media.

As with any study attempting to quantify qualitative content, to some degree the depth of each message was lost in those quantifying metrics. Additional attention to the role of intensifiers and differences in message strategies in the native language were not assessed. Future research focused on these efforts would enhance our understanding of message strategy use and effectiveness in a social media platform.

References

Ahmed, M. 2006. *The principles and practice of crisis management.* New York: Palgrave MacMillan.

African Union Mission in Somalia (AMISOM). n.d. www.amisom-au.org (Last modified 12 June 2012).

Ball, J. and R. Xan. 2011. Somalia famine appeal raises far less than previous disasters. *The Guardian,* 8 August.

Budd, R., R. Thorp and L. Donohew. 1967. *Content analysis of communications*. New York: Macmillan.

Beaubien, G. 2011. Facebook playing a vital but reticent role in Middle East revolts. *Public Relations Tactics* 18(3): 4.

Capelos, T. and J. Wurzer. 2009. United front: Blame management and scandal response tactics of the United Nations. *Journal of Contingencies and Crisis Management* 17(2): 75–94.

Christ, P. 2005. Internet technologies and trends transforming public relations. *Journal of Website Promotion* 1(4): 1–14.

Comunello, F. and G. Anzera. 2012. Will the revolution be tweeted? A conceptual framework for understanding the social media and the Arab Spring. *Islam & Christian-Muslim Relations* 23(4): 453–470.

Coombs, W.T. 2002. Deep and surface threats: Conceptual practical implications for 'crisis' vs. 'problems'. *Public Relations Review* 28(4): 339.

Coombs, W.T. 2006. The prospective powers of crisis response strategies: Managing reputation assets during a crisis. *Journal of Promotion Management* 12(3/4): 241–260.

Coombs, W.T. and S.J. Holladay. 2004. Reasoned action in crisis communication: An attribution theory-based approach to crisis management. In *Responding to crisis: A rhetorical approach to crisis communication*, ed. D.P. Millar and R.L. Heath, 95–115. Mahwah, NJ: Lawrence Erlbaum Associates.

Crowe, A. 2011. The social media manifesto: A comprehensive review of the impact of social media on emergency management. *Journal of Business Continuity & Emergency Planning* 5(1): 409–420.

Doctors Without Borders. 2011. Kenya: Fleeing Somalis struggle to find shelter at the world's largest refugee camp. *Field News*, 13 June.

Enda, J. 2011. Campaign coverage in the time of Twitter. *American Journalism Review* 33(2): 14–21.

Fearn-Banks, K. 2002. *Crisis communications: A casebook approach*, 2nd edition. Mahwah, NJ: Lawrence Erlbaum Associates.

Feldman, Major R. 2008 Problems plaguing the African Union peacekeeping forces. *Defense and Security Analysis* 24(3). 267–279.

Griswold, E. 2011. America's Somalia wake-up call. *The Daily Beast*, 17 July.

Jacques, A. 2011. 'On the ground': Pulitzer Prize-winner Kristof on covering crisis in the Middle East. *Public Relations Tactics* 18(4): 11.

Jurišić, J., I. Kanižaj, I. Jokoš, S. Janeš and J. Jurić. 2007. Manipulating readers: Disguised advertising in Croatian newspapers. *Politicka Misao: Croatian Political Science Review* 44(1): 117–135.

Kurokawa, D. 2011. Update: Aid for the food crisis in the horn of Africa – get the data. *The Guardian*, 1 August.

McCafferty, D. 2011. Brave, new social world. *Communications of the ACM* 54(7): 19–21.

McKaiser, E. 2012. Mind the UN–AU gap. Global opinion. *International Herald Tribune*, 8 January.

Mitroff, I.I. 2005. *Why some companies emerge stronger and better from a crisis: 7 essential lessons for surviving disaster.* New York: AMACOM.

Office for the Coordination of Humanitarian Affairs (OCHA). 2011. *Report on Somalia,* 27 September.

Oreskovic, A. 2010. Twitter snags over 100 million users, eyes money-making. *Reuters*, 4 April.

Reporters Without Borders. 2011. Somali radio presenter murdered. *The Guardian*, 8 August.

Samuels, B. 2011. Facebook, Twitter, YouTube – and democracy. *Academe* 97(4): n.p.

Savage, N. 2011. Twitter as medium and message. *Communications of the ACM* 54(3): 18–20.

Simmons, L.C. 2010. Disaster recovery: PR teams use networks to gather, share Haiti news. *Public Relations Tactics* 17(3): 18.

Smith, E. 1995. The new media and the emerging democracies of the Commonwealth. *Round Table* 334(1): 187.

Sutter, J.D. 2010. Twitter blames crashes on 'network equipment'. *CNNTech*, 10 June.

The African Union Commission. 2011. *Full report*, 29 October.

Tucker, C. 2011. Social media, texting play new role in response to disasters (cover story). *Nation's Health* 41(4): 1.

Warah, R. 2011. Manufacturing a famine: How Somalia crisis became a fund-raising opportunity. *The East African*, 2 October.

Wei, J., D. Zhao, F. Yang, S. Du and D. Marinova. 2010. Timing crisis information release via television. *Disasters* 34(4): 1013–1030.

Weimann, G. 2010. Terror on Facebook, Twitter and YouTube. *Brown Journal of World Affairs* 16(2): 45–54.

United Nations High Commission for Refugees (UNHCR). n.d. UNCHR, the UN refugee agency. www.unhcr.org/ (Last modified 23 October 2012).

A complicated but symbiotic affair: The relationship between mainstream media and social media in the coverage of social protests in southern Africa

Admire Mare

Abstract

Debates on the relationship between mainstream and social media have sputtered on in the academy, especially during crisis situations and social protests. Mostly based on conjecture and anecdotal evidence, there is little theorisation on the relationship between the two mediums in different contexts. Far from being competitors, mainstream and social media have converged in complex ways to broaden the mediated public sphere in southern Africa. While social media were instrumental in breaking news during social protests, mainstream media weighed in with verification, contextualisation and amplification. The convergence between the two public spheres has necessitated the emergence of collaborative journalism practices, making heard the voices of previously silenced and delegitimised activists.

Introduction

There seems to be consensus among scholars that the social media[1] offer an unprecedented space for ordinary people and journalists alike to both bypass and influence traditional information flows. Social media represent one of the latest fads in a long line of new media technologies, such as the Internet, email and mobile technology, which began to permeate newsrooms in the late 1990s. The rapid growth and permeation of social media in the everyday lives of different social classes in Africa have generated a bourgeoning scholarly interest. Questions abound about the extent to which the social media have supplemented or replaced traditional information sources; how social and other new media are being incorporated into journalism processes in Africa; to what extent social media have been an empowering force in Africa; and whether new forms of citizenship are emerging on the continent as a result of social media usage. In answering these questions, scholars tend to draw on utopian and dystopian views about the relationship between technology and society, and predictably arrive at diametrically opposed conclusions. The situation has been made worse by the prevalence of unsubstantiated generalisations, anecdotal case studies and an under-theorisation of the actually existing relationships between social and mainstream media[2] in different social contexts. Extant research conducted in Africa (Gaster 2010; Kuira and Makinen 2008; Mabweazara 2011; Moyo 2010) has focused on the creative appropriation of social media and mobile phones for political engagement, news gathering and distribution practices. For instance, during the Egyptian uprising, the interplay between social media and mainstream media allowed (some) traditional news consumers to become active participants in all stages of the production, dissemination and consumption of news, giving a voice to people who had previously been limited to more passive and non-interactive forms of news consumption. In the case of mobile technology, Mabweazara (2011, 693) argues that it has decentred the arena of newsmaking in Zimbabwe's mainstream press by offering an alternative avenue within the state-controlled and the private press. Citizen journalism has also contributed a great deal to the circulation of public opinion, and has to some extent influenced the way mainstream media covered the controversial 2008 elections in Zimbabwe (Moyo 2009). Similarly, in Kenya, during the 2007 post-electoral conflicts, the mainstream media relied heavily on Ushahidi-aggregated user-generated content (Makinen and Kuira 2008). On the other hand, exploratory research in the African context on citizen journalism suggests that conventional public and private media appear to underestimate or ignore the concept of citizen journalism (Banda 2010, 52–53). Their typical response has been to create online editions of their publications. Traditional media organisations in Africa are engrossed with absorbing citizen participation into classical formats (e.g. user blogging in mainstream newspapers), but clearly also show inclinations to restrict citizen journalism's function to that of news gathering, while professional journalists retain control over the entire process of selection, editing and presentation. As such, they exhibit a highly institutionalised approach to citizen journalism, tending to think of their newspapers as spaces for all citizens' contributions and suggestions.

This article explores the relationship between social and mainstream media in their coverage of the social protests that rocked Zimbabwe, Malawi and Mozambique. A brief overview of the current socio-political and economic context of the three countries is provided. Although southern Africa, unlike North Africa, has low Internet penetration, a short history of digital activism and underdeveloped telecommunications infrastructure (limited though rapidly increasing extra-urban mobile access and bandwidth in many areas), it nonetheless provides a good case for a close examination of the relationship under review here. Interestingly, in southern Africa, the latest wave of demonstrations has coincided with unprecedented popular revolts in North Africa (known as the 'Arab Spring'), with subsequent riots in London, and global demonstrations by the 'Occupy' movement. The three countries which are under consideration here have not been spared the recent wave of social protest (Commack

2011; Lloyd 2011; Manyozo 2012; Sachikonye 2009). Branded 'flawed democracies' (*Economic Intelligence Unit Report* 2011) they have experienced political crises of different natures and on varying scales. For instance, Zimbabwe has endured a decade of multilayered and multifaceted politico-economic crises (Mlambo and Raftopoulos 2010; Moyo 2009). Disputed elections and economic hardship have spawned running battles between ordinary citizens and political protagonists. Flash protests have often been the result of popular demands for better governance and improved living conditions, and have highlighted the inability of governments to satisfactorily respond to these demands (Mlambo and Raftopoulos 2010). Despite the swearing in of a government of national unity in 2008, Zimbabwe seems to be heading for a flawed transition, as evidenced by the slow resolution of outstanding issues: while the new government has managed to address issues pertaining to runaway inflation and economic instability, cosmetic political reforms have done little to consolidate or deepen democracy. ZANU-PF continues to control the levers of power, as evidenced by the unilateral appointment of the Attorney General, the Governor of the Reserve Bank of Zimbabwe, provincial governors and ambassadors. Malawi, on the other hand, graced international news headlines for all the wrong reasons, under the tutelage of the late President Bingu wa Mutharika. The country experienced bad political and economic governance characterised by the narrowing of the democratic space, media repression and jobless economic growth since 2009 (Commack 2011; Manyozo 2012). When fuel and foreign currency shortages drove the masses into the streets in July 2011, the government reacted harshly by deploying the military. While the elevation of Joyce Banda to the position of president of Malawi has generally been hailed as having drawn back the country from an economic and political precipice, transition without transformation remains a serious challenge. Mozambique emerged from years of bitter civil war in 1992 and quickly revoked its Marxist socialist leanings by embracing neoliberal economic policies (Lloyd 2011). The country has won many admirers for its stable political and economic system, yet on the surface its superficial stability and prosperity (for a few and for the politically well-connected) have masked widespread social and economic disparities that threaten what passes for peaceful rule (Jacobs and Duarte 2010). This brief hiatus came to an end in September 2010, following a sudden rise in the cost of living, when trade unions and grassroots social movements picketed on bread and butter issues.

The death of journalism? Advocates and opponents of social media

Spawned by new media technologies in various forms (Banda 2010), citizen journalism is widely seen as heralding a new era where the power to define what is news has been recast and decentred (Moyo 2009, 553). However, Banda (2010, 9) cautions against viewing new media technologies as enablers of citizen journalism. The argument here is that, although citizen journalism is generally associated with the Internet, it does not begin and end online or even with digital-interactive media (Goode 2009). Given that citizen journalism is a relatively new phenomenon, the boundaries of its definition have not been completely settled (Lasica 2003). Some scholars define citizen journalism 'as news of the people, by the people and for the people' (Banda 2010, 7), while others see it as 'a philosophy of journalism and a set of practices that are embedded within the everyday lives of citizens, and media content that is both driven and produced by those people . . . (and whose) practices emphasise first person, eyewitness accounts by participants' (Atton 2003, 267). The overarching thread running through most of these definitions is that citizen journalists gather, process, research, report, analyse and publish news and information, most often utilising a variety of technologies made possible by the Internet (Goode 2009, 1288; Ross and Cormier 2010, 66). Included here is 'metajournalism' (Dvorak 2006), which encompasses practices such as rating, commenting, tagging and reposting. In summary, it encapsulates practices such as current affairs-based blogging, photo and video sharing, and posting eyewitness commentary on current events. Given the deliberative or participatory turn engendered by social media, Hermida (2010) sees citizen journalism as synonymous with social or participatory journalism, which encompasses the generation of content by users for users, and the devolution of all the different steps of news gathering, selection, editing and distribution to ordinary, non-professional citizens. Moyo (2010) and Goode (2009) write that in Africa, journalism has always existed alongside other forms of news dissemination and storytelling. In the same vein, Steenveld and Strelitz (2010) warn against the wholesale borrowing and adoption of the Western model of citizen journalists as 'produsers' (Bruns 2007). This view presumes a citizenry of both consumers and producers of media products, who are relatively well educated, and are familiar with, and have access to, the new media as a form of social communication. In addition, they are confident of their right to participate in newly-developed public spheres, particularly those that are online. Another cautionary remark is that 'these technologies can be seen both as agents of inclusion and exclusion in terms of citizen participation' (Moyo 2009).

Although the advent of new media technologies in Africa in the 1990s 'sparked celebratory, almost utopian bliss' (Banda et al. 2009, 1), one of its offspring, citizen journalism, has met with strong opposition and criticism from media commentators (Anderson 2005; Hermida 2009). In Europe and America, 'prophets of doom' have announced the imminent death of journalism, while others have already composed funeral dirges such as the infamous '*Long live journalism, print is eternal*'. Much of the public debate on the relationship between social media and journalism has taken place within the trenches of the blogosphere, largely due to the slow speed at which academic wheels turn. Anderson (2005) captures this cynicism as follows: 'Faced with the challenge of analyzing the impact of the internet and its various journalistic stepchildren – on traditional forms of news gathering and reporting, media commentators tend to adopt an unfortunate all-or-nothing rhetoric.' McNair (2009, 347–348), however, reassuringly states: 'Journalism will not die out in this environment, because it is needed on so many social, political and cultural levels. Journalism has a future.' Most alarmistic critiques of the perceived impact of social media on journalism have fallen into the trap of technological determinism, which downplays the role of political and social factors, and hence they suffer from the poverty of nuanced analysis. As McNair (2009, 347) insightfully observes, 'the future of journalism is often conflated with the future of a particular journalistic medium, currently print'. While newspapers are in crisis in advanced capitalist societies, it must be noted that circulation figures are expanding in India and other developing countries.

The reaction of 'moral panic' against citizen journalism (as against tabloids before that) is promoted by journalists and news organisations whose loud and strident voices warn of the growth of slacktivism (the act of participating in obviously pointless activities as an expedient alternative to actually expending effort to fix a problem) and noise within the communication ecosystem. For Hermida (2010), current academic debates on how the social media complement or compete against journalism often turn into legitimation battles about whether the 'de facto' solution is a social media network rather than a media institution. Such debates serve to police the boundaries of the profession by reiterating accepted definitions of what it is to be a journalist. When these boundaries are transgressed, the paradigm is threatened (Wasserman 2005). In terms of theoretical debates on the interplay between journalism and social media, three broad categories are identifiable: 1) supporters who hail the democratic virtues of the social media; 2) detractors who critique the social media for creating problems for journalism; and 3) those who advocate a middle-ground approach to promote synergies between the 'fourth' and the 'fifth' estates. Supporters of citizen journalism see it as an opportunity to 'democratise' rather than 'deprofessionalise' journalism. Social media are deemed to introduce a new dimension to journalism by allowing a space for contributions and opinions. They are credited with giving people an opportunity to voice their own thoughts and opinions – something traditional media platforms lack. Social media are seen as changing our traditional 'just-the-facts-Ma'am' attitude to news, as supplementing coverage and uncovering under-represented topics and stories in the mainstream press. Advocates of citizen journalism point to its instrumental role during the Queensland floods in Australia (Bruns and Burgess 2010; Posetti 2011), the riots in Iran (Hermida 2010), the 2010 Haitian earthquake crisis (Bruno 2011) and the Arab Spring (Harlow and Johnson 2011; Newman 2011). According to proponents of citizen journalism, interactive media applications clearly democratise representation by making it a more direct relationship: as citizens gain access to inexpensive communication technologies, the gatekeeping monopoly editors and broadcasters once enjoyed, is waning. New media technologies have revised the circuit of culture through the convergence of the production and the consumption of news. This occurs not merely through passive bespoke consumption, but through active engagement via blogging, re-posting, commenting, recommending, rating, tagging and the like. Far from cannibalising news and media traffic, social media are helping media organisations to direct traffic to news sites (Newman 2011).

Opponents of citizen journalism accuse it of undermining the philosophical foundations of journalism, i.e. promoting unethical conduct and undermining gatekeeping control over content. Social media are also castigated for destabilising 'tried and tested' business models through their promotion of 'free online news'. As Newman (2011, 10) argues, 'social media are changing the production, distribution and discovery of news and further disrupting the business models of mainstream media companies'. Facebook and Twitter stand accused of living parasitically off the quality content produced by mainstream media and reaping the commercial benefit. Even more scathing has been criticism voiced against the quality and reliability of information available on Facebook and Twitter, along with the dumbing down of the agenda of information, while others point to new perspectives opening up (McNair 2009). There are fears that the filtering of news sources through friends and colleagues could minimise diversity and reinforce prejudices (Sunstein 2011). Detractors regard the social media as an 'invasive weed' with the power to 'deprofessionalise' journalism. Newman (2011) describes the acrimonious relationship between social media and journalism as a clash of style and cultures over the unregulated, anything-goes nature of the peer-to-peer Internet. Despite these seemingly different epistemological roots, mainstream journalism and citizen journalism complement each other in a myriad of ways. For instance, broadcast news often feeds off and incorporates elements of citizen journalism through the use of eyewitness footage from cell phones, the reporting of stories originally broken by citizen journalism initiatives on the web, or even guest reporter slots in which citizens participate in packaging an item for a television or radio newscast. A middle-ground perspective has been offered by a number of scholars who see the social media as fostering 'collaborative reporting' (Hermida 2010), which reincarnates the notion of 'public' or 'civic' journalism (Rosen 2001). At the core of public journalism is the belief that 'journalism has an obligation to public life – an obligation that goes beyond just telling the news or unloading lots of facts. The way we do our journalism affects the way public life goes. Journalism can help empower a community or it can help disable it.' To journalistic reformers, reporting has always been something of a collaborative process between journalists and their sources. The social media are hailed for blowing open the editorial office doors and demanding a conversation, not just a response. Reflecting on the 'Twitterisation of journalism', Posetti (2010) contends that the use of Twitter makes journalism more openly reflective and interactive. Far from being arch rivals, the Internet and social media are actually helping to achieve some of the core goals of journalism: strengthening society, communities and democracy, in part through sharing information (PEW Internet Research 2011).

Methodological approach

This article analyses the relationship between mainstream and social media in their coverage of social protests in southern Africa, in light of trends witnessed during the North African uprisings, where mainstream news organisation such as Al Jazeera relied heavily on social media for news gathering and distribution (Newman 2011). In view of the foregoing, this study sought to address two research questions:

- To what extent did the mainstream media trail social media or vice versa during the southern African protests, especially in Zimbabwe, Malawi and Mozambique?
- How were social media platforms incorporated into processes of journalism during the coverage of the recent protests in southern Africa?

To answer the above research questions, this study adopted a qualitative research methodology. Data were largely gathered through documentary searches, in-depth interviews and qualitative content analyses. Qualitative content analysis was used for gathering and analysing the content of texts posted on social network sites during the protests (Deacon et al. 1999). In-depth interviews were useful in obtaining journalists' views on how they gathered news and where they sourced news, and to interrogate how both mainstream and social media fed into and off each other. Several key informants were contacted for their informed views on the relationship between the mainstream and social media in terms of their coverage of social protests in Malawi, Mozambique and Zimbabwe. Thus, key informants were chosen through purposive sampling and based on their ability to provide rich data.

Tweet/post first and verify later vs. verify first and publish later: The relationship between journalism and social media in coverage of protests in southern Africa

The findings of this study demonstrate that social media played a complementary and supplementary role to the mainstream media, through their real-time news feeds, viral videos and participatory news-making practices. In fact, in the three countries studied, the social media did not try to replace the mainstream media, but merely provided an alternative public sphere for activists and ordinary citizens. This is in stark contrast to assertions which claim that the old and the new media are rivals or competitors. Mainstream and social media worked together in synergy to create a stronger, more resilient and better networked information system. In the case of Malawi, the mainstream media trailed behind the social media in their coverage of the 20 July protests. Private and community radio stations relied on Facebook posts and Twitter feeds to disseminate early warning information. In Mozambique, the social media were responsible for breaking news, while newspapers and television stations resorted to curating information from social network sites, in order to follow up on developing stories. In Zimbabwe, the social media and mobile telephony were newsworthy for breaking the news. Even diasporic media (such as clandestine radio stations and online newspapers) raided updates on the mobilisation of protests, from social media platforms. The situation was made more precarious by state media blackouts imposed in all three countries, which forced ordinary citizens to source breaking and developing news on the 'parallel market of information' (Moyo 2009). Citizen journalists filled up the information vacuum created by the temporary bans imposed on live radio broadcasts in Malawi and on telecommunications services in Mozambique. In response to the bans, citizen journalists outside the two countries took it upon themselves to maintain the momentum, using social media and mobile phones to bridge geographical barriers and maintain the coverage of events in the virtual sphere. Citizen journalism and community media were instrumental in providing 'alternative' avenues of news production, distribution and consumption in Malawi and Mozambique. While activists-cum-citizen journalists resorted to social media to self-represent their narratives, professional journalists followed influential activists on social media platforms for breaking and developing news. Thus, the 'professional variable' in the coverage of protests in Malawi and Mozambique entwined, overlapped and mixed with the 'amateur variable'. Unlike professional journalists who continued with their time-honoured approach of 'verify first and publish later', citizen journalists resorted to a 'tweet/post first and verify later' approach. The different approaches ensured that the mainstream media trailed the social media as regards the coverage of social protests in southern Africa. Given their respect for their professional obligations, professional journalists lagged behind citizen journalists in breaking news. This is because citizen journalists are under no professional obligation to uphold the time-honoured ethics of journalism and are not constrained by traditional journalistic processes or routines, but usually function without editorial oversight.

The mainstream media trailed the social media in terms of breaking up-to-the-minute news in the three countries studied. In Mozambique, residents of Maputo, who took to the streets, were prompted by SMS (short message service) to 'enjoy the great day of the strike' and to 'protest the increase in energy, water, mini-bus taxi and bread prices'. During these SMS-organised protests, journalists and ordinary citizens used Twitter to report on-the-ground news to a global audience. They also uploaded links to their stories, photos, videos and blogs. Twitter was mostly used by foreign news agencies and local journalists (such as Erik Charas and Jorge Barata) to source news and connect with a global audience. The following tweet sums up the relationship between the social and the mainstream media during the riots in Maputo: 'Hello, how can we contact you to talk about Maputo riots? Please come back to us,' Schmitt tweeted. The tweet was addressed to @JorgeBarata from freelance journalist Amandine Schmitt on behalf of the *Observers* news blog run by France 24. Similarly, Charas received a tweet from Faith Karimi, a CNN International Wire news desk editor (@FaithCNN): 'Are you in Maputo? Can you DM a phone contact I can reach you for a story?' Besides recruiting sources on social media, on-the-ground reporters such as South African, Nastasya Tay, used her Twitter feed to convey the perils and moment-to-moment uncertainty of the unfolding chaos in Maputo. One of her tweets read as follows: 'Armoured trucks patrolling the street and shooting at unarmed crowds. Phone stolen in riot so belated tweets.' A few hours later she tweeted: 'Windy morning in Maputo. The sound of an unexpected lone trumpeter rings out over the city. What does today hold?' While the state media chose to continue with their normal programming, videos appearing on YouTube illustrated different aspects of the riots, from police action to looting, and in turn provoked more commentary. The social media provided a space for many voices and opinions to be heard, while television and radio stations tended to rely on the same pool of analysts for their studio debates and news programmes (Gaster 2010). In their complementary roles, the mainstream media were instrumental in verifying, contextualising and amplifying information, as corroborated in this interview extract:

> *In Maputo, Facebook played a very important role in disseminating accurate information about the riots that started on September 1st. While I was watching what was happening in two local TV broadcasters, through Facebook I was being updated virtually by the second by people who were located in various parts of town. At the same time, I knew exactly what was going on in 7 or 8 streets of Maputo. Journalists could not do this especially in Mozambique. People turned*

to Facebook to know which road they should use to pick up their kids from school when the riots started, or to return home safely. Some used it to assess whether or not it was safe to go to work on the second day of social unrest in Maputo.

In Zimbabwe, the rise of the Internet, social media and mobile phone has presented alternative means of communication to the state-owned media (Ndlela 2009). Although the establishment of the government of national unity has seen the licensing and relicensing of private newspapers and radio stations, draconian media laws are still in place. Recent protests in Zimbabwe, organised by the Mthwakazi Liberation Front (MLF) and Women of Zimbabwe Arise (WOZA), were covered by private newspapers, clandestine radio stations and online newspapers. Social media platforms were instrumental in breaking the news during the preparation phase and also in amplifying news raided from the mainstream media. In Zimbabwe, Facebook has become a means of criticising dictatorship, corruption and censorship – in short, a space in which to challenge the regime. As one journalist commented:

> *Given the repressive actions of the police in Zimbabwe, most organisers of protests are increasingly publicising their demonstrations online before the mainstream media catches the wind of it. Online newspapers and pirate radio stations have also become indispensable news breakers. Although social media are increasingly making news for breaking news in Zimbabwe, traditional news outlets still have a key role to play in providing investigation and context into issues. The relationship between social and mainstream media is like that of fish and water. Both are essential in the sense that they enable us to gain a full picture of events. Whereas the other is constrained by political and economic factors, the other is characterised by unfettered audience participation and unending threads of conversation. In the end, social media covers up for the weaknesses of the mainstream media through real time and seamless news updates.*

In Malawi, details of demonstrations were circulated via Facebook, Twitter, mass emailing and online newspapers. Days prior to the demonstration, Twitter was abuzz with hashtags #july20 and #redarmy. While 20 July refers to the day scheduled for the demonstrations, #redarmy refers to the red shirts the protestors wore. For instance, @DutchessCarol tweeted: 'Everyone who was in the streets was to wear red as a symbol of solidarity. Red stands for flames, which is the English name for Malawi.' Furthermore, a respected editor at The Nation Newspapers Group, Mabvuto Banda, commented: 'In Malawi, Facebook, Twitter and other social media tools were used to show the whole world the brutal nature of Mutharika's police and PMF. People upload content on Facebook, YouTube and Twitter in real-time.' Through status updates, people were able to call others to act, disseminate information, and express their sentiments on the issues at hand. The banning of radio live broadcasts by the Malawi Communications Regulatory Authority (MACRA) forced journalists, protestors and ordinary citizens alike to start using social media tools to publicise human rights violations. As Kaonga (2011) observes, 'on Wednesday 20th July, many who have access to Facebook and Twitter were online sharing updates'. He adds that the ban on live radio broadcasts of the demonstrations left the people with no choice but go online. In this way, social media allowed those far away – whether members of a diasporic community living outside Malawi or members of an international audience – to follow events literally in real-time. During the 20 July protests most journalists actively participated as bloggers and citizen journalists. The mainstream media tapped into social network sites and online newspapers for topics and sources for their stories. A number of journalists interviewed aptly captured the relationship between the mainstream media and social media as follows:

> *The protests began to 'trend' on Twitter-South Africa before they made the news headlines. Ordinary Malawians had proceeded to tweet directly to BBC, Anderson Cooper, CNN, and Sky News during the course of the day to ensure that international attention would be brought on the demonstrations. By day two, Malawi protests began to 'trend' as a hot topic on Google. The online community engaged directly with programs like BBC-Have Your Say (BBCHYS) and France 24, acting much like a watchdog to ensure that the international media was going to cover the protests and was going to cover it with accuracy.*

> *During the demonstrations online newspapers such as NyasaTimes.com and Face of Malawi were ahead of print newspapers in terms of breaking the news. They took advantage of their underground reporters who have sources in high government offices to report and upload content in real time. Social media platforms like Facebook were used by the urban youth to post eyewitness accounts. In fact, during that time I remember everyone in the newsroom used to read Nyasa Times and Face of Malawi before the diary meeting in order to get news tips.*

From the extracts above, it is clear that social media, online newspapers and mobile technologies played a central role in the way stories are sourced, broken and distributed, thus helping to further speed up the news cycle. The symbiotic relationship between the social media and private radio stations ensured source diversification and led to richer coverage of the protests in the three countries. The overreliance on social media for breaking news by the 'mainstream media outlets heightened the decentralized character of the protest-related communications, fuelling the power of the margins rather than the centre in the communications war, effectively adding another front in the circumvention of media control'. As intimated earlier, the difference in approaches, where social media adopted the 'tweet/post first and verify later' approach whereas mainstream media continued with 'verify first and publish later' explain the reasons why the latter lagged behind. Again, whereas the mainstream news organisations were constrained by news production cycles, social media operated on the principle of 'news is like fish, it goes bad quickly' (Mare 2009). In the age of digitisation, where production and consumption occur simultaneously, social media's 'post/tweet first and verify later' gives it a comparative advantage in breaking news. With the mainstream media controlled and dominated by the government in Malawi, Zimbabwe and Mozambique, social media constituted 'alternative communicative spaces independent of the cohesive apparatus of the state' (Ndlela 2009, 94). As Newman (2011, 55) notes, social media behave as a 'selective amplifier for the content generated by the mainstream media, with chains of retweets and posts by many users helping the content to go viral'. This in addition to being an alternative source of news, the social media act more as a filter and an amplifier for interesting news from the mainstream media.

Creative appropriation of social media platforms

The influences of digitisation, the Internet, mobile communications and the social media are forcing newsrooms to adapt in various ways. It is clear from this study that 'far from being mired in "backwardness" or passively awaiting external salvation in regard to attempts to creatively use new media technologies, African media organisations are incorporating social media platforms into processes of news gathering and distribution'. Internal newsroom cultures and creativity, in conjunction with the wider socio-political and economic circumstances in which professional and citizen journalists operate, have shaped the creative appropriation of new media technologies in the three countries studied. It is important to point out that when compared to commercial news organisations, the community and diasporic media embraced the social media as 'portals of news gathering, processing, and distributing information'. This was evidenced by their active presences on Facebook and Twitter, which allow them to 'stay plugged in to the changing needs of consumers – consumers who now demand around-the-clock access to news' (Hermida 2010). In the case of Zimbabwe and Mozambique, most newspapers and radio stations have appropriated social media and SMS as channels for interacting directly with readers, viewers and listeners (Gaster 2010; Moyo 2009). For instance, Verdade publishes Facebook posts and SMS in its weekly newspaper. In Zimbabwe, the *Zimbabwe Standard*, the *Zimbabwe Independent*, *The Herald* and *NewsDay* carry a section where SMS messages from readers are printed. Moyo (2009) adds that even the most prominent 'clandestine' of radio stations beaming into Zimbabwe, *SW Radio Africa*, uses SMS to obtain news tips and send news headlines to subscribers. As Bruno (2011, 65) observes, this strategy seems 'very dangerous for one of journalism's golden rules: each news story must be verified first'. Writing about the notion of citizen journalism in Zimbabwe, Moyo (2009, 562) reminds us that 'it is not necessarily emerging as a distinct form of "unmediated" space of communication, but rather as a hybrid form, as mainstream media increasingly tap into that space as a way of creating a certain impression about their close links to the citizenry as testimony of citizen engagement'.

From personal conversations with professional journalists in Zimbabwe, Malawi and Mozambique, it emerged that social media platforms were being incorporated into processes of news gathering and distribution, for a myriad of reasons, including to uncover news tips; gather content for stories; pursue and build news sources; reach out and connect with news sources; friend and follow influential activists; discuss future events; gauge the public mood about events on the ground; report and clarify rumours; create and circulate stories; and explore significant comments and replies in order to get more updates and interact with a broad section of citizens. During the social protests in southern Africa, individual journalists defied newsroom rules on social media usage, for instance, in Malawi citizen journalists 'scooped' 'the Fourth Estate' with immediate eyewitness footage, while professional journalists also raided 'the Fifth Estate' for 'scoops'. Zodiak Broadcasting Services (ZBS), a private radio station, was popular for its appropriation of Facebook posts throughout the demonstrations in Malawi. In Mozambique, Verdade experimented with Ushahidi during the riots in Maputo, which enabled the community newspaper to harness as much on-the-ground news as possible, compared to traditional news-gathering methods. Respondents described the creative appropriation of social media by mainstream media organisations as follows:

> Social media have become eyes and ears of the mainstream media. In places, where news organisations have no correspondents, ordinary citizens are taking it upon themselves to file cellphone footage accompanied with captions and stories. Since we pioneered the concept of citizen journalism during the 2010 riots in Maputo, we have followed it up by introducing the Facebook wall just outside our gate. It is black board curated on the durawall in front of our offices. Everyone can come and post anything newsworthy happening in their neighbourhood. Through this platform, we allow ordinary people to collaborate with our journalists in the news making process.

> Radio stations were periodically checking on their Facebook pages for updates on the situation on the ground in certain areas, and then inform people to avoid dangerous places. Instead of relying on newspapers to publish news, DJs resorted to sourcing news from Twitter, Facebook and online newspapers such as NyasaTimes.com. Private radio stations carried live coverage which gave the public almost minute-to-minute account of the events on the streets of the country. This information was vital as it kept the public abreast of what was going on and helped them make informed decisions and security precautions.

> I remember that day i was going to work and i saw rioters blocking roads leading to Maputo with huge boulders, stones and burning tyres. I only had my cellphone so i decided to use it to capture the demonstrations. I also contacted the editor to dispatch journalists to the scene and other parts in Matola and Maputo where demonstrations were taking place. We posted news in real time on Facebook, Twitter and YouTube and before long we were joined by fellow citizens who contributed content on our social network sites profile pages. Initially there was no central command system to coordinate content distribution but the way individuals from all walks of life collaborated online was unprecedented. Verdade also made use of Ushahidi which proved instrumental in crowd sourcing content and mapping human rights abuses by the police in Maputo.

Social media thus facilitate a type of journalism in which the audience is much more involved in the news-creation process. It allows ordinary citizens to participate in the news-gathering processes by actively soliciting user-generated content and publishing it in mainstream media. The social and the mainstream media co-exist in a symbiotic relationship, feeding off and amplifying each other. Traditional mainstream media continue to drive the majority of news conversations in social media (Newman 2011). Although during the recent protests in Malawi news first emerged via Twitter and Facebook, it was the mainstream media that picked up on it and packaged it for a mass audience. In such collaborative reporting, there is a need for professional journalists to embrace non-professional newcomers by treating them as knowledgeable actors. Journalism, as a team-work profession, can benefit greatly from non-professional newcomers in an age of 24-hour news cycles.

Conclusion

The findings presented in this article point to the fact that the relationship between journalism and social media is complex. Throughout the four phases of the social protests (preparation, ignition, escalation and post-protests), the social media made a profound difference in terms of breaking news, while the mainstream media weighed in with verification, contextualisation and amplification. Thus the 'Fifth Estate' and the 'Fourth Estate' fed off each other in complex ways which highlight journalistic and citizens' agency in both repressive and democratic contexts. The fact that professional journalists in southern Africa took their cues from social media platforms points to the growing importance of citizens as information producers and disseminators. It also showed how, during recent political protests in southern Africa, the social media functioned as an alternative public sphere for both citizen and professional journalists. In the end, collaborative journalistic practices emerged which enabled both professional and non-professional journalists to execute their watchdog role with relative ease. Democratising journalistic practice does not necessarily mean the erosion of vital values of the profession, such as truth-telling, fairness and balance. In fact, the democratisation of journalism leads to a new form of objectivity which foregrounds transparency, honesty and the ethic of the everyday, while giving a voice to the voiceless.

Acknowledgements

This study was made possible by generous funding from the Open Society Initiative of Southern Africa (OSISA) and the Highway Africa Chair of Media and Information Society based at Rhodes University, South Africa. It was part of a regional study on activists' use of social media during recent protests which rocked southern Africa (Zimbabwe, South Africa, Swaziland, Mozambique and Malawi). While their support is gratefully acknowledged, the views reflected in this study are those of the author and not the two funding organisations.

Notes

1   For the present purposes, a broader definition of social media is: 'Websites which build on Web 2.0 technologies to provide space for in-depth social interaction, community formation, and the tackling of collaborative projects' (Bruns and Bahnisch 2009, 5).

2   The dominant model of journalism in the 20th century is based on the normative understanding of the mainstream media and their role in a democracy, as espoused in the Habermasian public sphere theory. From this perspective, the media have an important role to play in creating a public space for discussion and dissent (Golding and Murdock 2000). Journalism was the preserve of the few, and was delivered by an authoritative public voice, where authority was determined by consensually accepted forms of organisational, professional and cultural status (McNair 2009).

References

Anderson, C. 2005. *An analysis of online journalism, professionalism, and the role of expert knowledge in the collection of news.* 16 December. http:www.indymedia.org/DeprofJourn.pdf (accessed 28 September 2009).

Atton, C. 2003. What is alternative journalism? *Journalism* 4(3): 267–272.

Banda, F. 2010. *Citizen journalism and democracy in Africa: An exploratory study.* Grahamstown: Highway Africa.

Boyd, D.M. and N.B. Ellison. 2007. Social network sites: Definition, history, and scholarship. *Journal of Computer-Mediated Communication* 13(1). http://jcmc.indiana.edu/vol13/issue1/ boyd.ellison.html (accessed 22 November 2010).

Bruns, A. 2007. Produsage: Towards a broader framework for user-led content creation. http://www. siteseerx.ist.psu.edu (accessed 31 July 2010).

Bruns, A. and M. Bahnisch. 2009. *Social media: Tools for user-generated content social drivers behind growing consumer participation in user-led content generation.* Eveleigh: Smart Services CRC.

Bruns, A. and J. Burgess. 2011. Twitter, crisis, and authority: The role of @QPSMedia during the Queensland floods. Paper presented at the Association of Internet Researchers Conference, 10–13 October, Seattle, WA.

Bruno, N. 2011. *Tweet first, verify later? How real-time information is changing the coverage of worldwide crisis events.* Reuters Institute for the Study of Journalism Report, University of Oxford. Michaelmas and Hilary Term 2010–2011. Oxford: Thomson Reuters Foundation.

Cammack, D. 2011. *Malawi's political settlement in crisis.* Background paper 4. London: The Africa Power and Politics Programme (APPP) and Overseas Development Institute.

Deacon, D., P. Golding, G. Murdock and M. Pickering. 1999. *Researching communications: A practical guide to methods in media and cultural analysis.* New York: Hodder.

Dvorak, J.C. 2006. Citizen journalism is like citizen professional baseball: You can't play pro baseball just because you think the Seattle Mariners Stink. *PC Magazine* 25(18): 1–10.

Economic Intelligence Unit. 2011. *Democracy index 2011: Democracy under stress.* A report. London: The Economist Intelligence Unit Limited.

Freedom House. 2011. *The authoritarian challenge to democracy: Selected data from Freedom House's annual survey of political rights and civil liberties.* New York: Freedom House.

Gaster, P. 2011. Mozambique Report, Year: 2011 – Internet rights and democratisation. http://www. giswatch//mozambique (accessed 19 January 2012).

Goode, L. 2009. Social news, citizen journalism and democracy. *New Media & Society* 11: 1287–1305.

Goode, L., A. McCullough and G. O'Hare. 2011. Unruly publics and the Fourth Estate on YouTube. *Journal of Audience and Reception Studies* 8(2): 594–615.

Gordon, J. 2007.The mobile phone and the public sphere: Mobile phone usage in three critical situations – convergence. *The International Journal of Research into New Media Technologies* 13(3): 307–319.

Habermas, J. 1989. *The structural transformation of the public sphere: An inquiry into a category of bourgeois society.* Cambridge, MA: MIT Press.

Harlow, S. and J.T. Johnson. 2011. Overthrowing the protest paradigm? How *The New York Times*, global voices and Twitter covered the Egyptian Revolution. *International Journal of Communication* 5: 1359–1374.

Hermida, A. 2010. Twittering the news: The emergence of ambient journalism. *Journalism Practice* 4(3): 1–12.

Jacobs, S. and D. Duarte. 2010, 16 September. Protests in Mozambique: The power of SMS. www. afronline.com (accessed 20 March 2012).

Kaonga, V. 2011, 25 July. When the social media also protested in Malawi. CIVICUS World Assembly. http://www.citizenshift.org (accessed 15 April 2012).

Keita, M. 2010. New media tools bring Mozambican crisis to the world. http://cpj.org/blog/2010/09/ new-media-brings-crisis-in-mozambique-to-the-world.php (accessed 25 February 2012).

Lewis, S.C. 2010. Journalism innovation and the ethic of participation: A case study of the Knight Foundation and its news challenge. Unpublished dissertation, University of Texas, Austin.

Lloyd, R. 2011. *Countries at the crossroads 2011: Mozambique.* New York: Freedom House.

Mabweazara, H.M. 2010. Newsmaking practices and professionalism in the Zimbabwean Press. *Journalism Practice* 5(1): 100–117.

Makinen, M. and W.M. Kuira. 2008. Social media and postelection crisis in Kenya. *The International Journal on Press/Politics* 13: 328–335.

Manyozo, L. 2012. Can the Malawian 'vendors' speak? http:/www.nyasatimes.com/ Malawi/2012/01/19/can-the-malawian-vendors speak/stripped_women_in_dresses-bus_banner (accessed 26 January 2012).

Mare, A. 2009. Facebooking the Zimbabwean crisis: Reclaiming or reinventing the public sphere – the case of Zimbabweans living in the diaspora. Paper presented at SACOMM Conference, Communication and Media: Past, Present and Future, 26–29 September, North-West University, Potchefstroom.

McNair, B. 2009. Journalism in the 21st century – evolution, not extinction. *Journalism* 10(3): 347– 349.

Mlambo, A. and B. Raftopoulos. 2010. The regional dimensions of the Zimbabwe's multi-layered crisis: An analysis. Paper presented at the Election Processes, Liberation Movements and Democratic Change in Africa Conference, 8–11 April, Maputo, Mozambique (CIM and IESE).

Moyo, D. 2009. Citizen journalism and the parallel market of information in Zimbabwe's 2008 election. *Journalism Studies* 10(4): 551–567.

Murdock, G. and P. Golding. 2000. Culture, communication and political economy. In *Mass media and society*, 3rd edition, ed. J. Curran and M. Gurevitch, 52–80. London: Arnold.

Newman, N. 2009. *The rise of social media and its impact on mainstream journalism.* London: Reuters Institute for the Study of Journalism.

Newman, N. 2011. *Mainstream media and the distribution of news in the age of social discovery.* London: Reuters Institute for the Study of Journalism.

Ndlela, M.N. 2009. *Alternative media and the political public sphere in Zimbabwe.* In *Understanding community media*, ed. K. Howley, 87–95. London: Sage.

Nyamnjoh, F.B. 2010. Racism, ethnicity and the media in Africa: Reflections inspired by studies of xenophobia in Cameroon and South Africa. *Africa Spectrum* 45(1): 57–93.

Pavlik, J. 2001. *Journalism and new media.* New York: Columbia University Press.

Posetti, J. 2010. Twitterising journalism and J-Ed: An Australian political reporting case study. Paper presented at the World Journalism Education Congress, 5–7 July, Grahamstown, South Africa.

Posetti, J. 2012. The Twitterisation of ABC's emergency and disaster communication. *The Australian Journal of Emergency Management* 27(1): 34–39.

Ross, R. and S.C. Cormier. 2010. *Handbook for citizen journalists.* Denver, CO: National Association of Citizen Journalists (NACJ).

Steenveld, L. and L. Strelitz. 2010. Citizen journalism in Grahamstown: *Iindaba Ziyafika* and the difficulties of instituting citizen journalism in a poor South African country town. Paper presented at the World Journalism Education Congress, 5–7 July, Grahamstown, South Africa.

Sunstein, C. 2009. *On rumours: How falsehoods spread, why we believe them, what can be done.* New York: Farrar, Strauss and Giroux.

Wasserman, H. 2005. A 'danger to journalism'. *Rhodes Journalism Review* 25: 34–35.

Wasserman, H. 2012. The ethics of the everyday: Towards cultural normativity of the South African media. Paper presented at the Beyond Normative Approaches: Everyday Media Culture in Africa Conference, 27–29 February, University of the Witwatersrand, Johannesburg.

Case studies from southern Africa

Chris Paterson

In compiling this special issue, the editor was privileged to read a variety of innovative research concerning social and online media in Africa, some of which represented smaller projects or work in progress, and so would not normally have qualified for publication as full research articles. Three such projects are presented here, including one co-authored by the issue editor. The authors were asked to present the work in an abbreviated form, with a focus on specific cases of social and online media use in the three southern African countries they have examined: Swaziland, Mozambique and Zimbabwe. In each country there is mounting evidence of mobile telephony, collaborative online communication, and social media becoming increasingly significant as influences on and adjuncts to traditional journalism, and as tools of political mobilisation for disenfranchised and/or disempowered populations, but these small case studies reach differing conclusions on their potential. These cases usefully extend the overview of the mainstream media and social media relationship in southern Africa provided by Mare, earlier in this issue.

Social media and journalism: The case of Swaziland

Richard Charles Rooney

Swaziland is a small kingdom landlocked between Mozambique and South Africa, where King Mswati III rules as sub-Saharan Africa's only remaining absolute monarch (US State Department 2011). Content published by mainstream news media is severely restricted by law and the custom of self-censorship (Freedom House 2011a). In recent years, social media have become significant for their distribution of information and ideas that are not available elsewhere. In particular, they offer spaces to advocate the democratisation of the political system in Swaziland. This brief contribution examines the state of social media in Swaziland, with particular reference to how they are increasing established flows of information 1) for people who live in Swaziland to communicate with one another and 2) by allowing those outside the kingdom to contribute to discussions in support of democratic change. Such information includes outright criticism of King Mswati III and the royal family; details about pro-democracy events, protests and strikes; and commentary and discussion that draw attention to the need for democratic reform in Swaziland.

This research addressed two research questions: Are the social media changing established flows of information in and about Swaziland, and to what extent have the social media been an empowering force in Swaziland? The author concludes that although there are clearly additional flows of information about the need for political change in Swaziland, there is little evidence that social media sites are empowering people to effect that change.

To counter the restriction imposed on and by media as regards information in Swaziland, a number of social media sites have emerged in recent years. This has been a relatively slow development, because although in Swaziland the number of people using the Internet is growing, totals are low. The Internet World Stats website reports that only 6.9 per cent of the population (95 122 people) were Internet users in Swaziland as at 31 December 2011 (Internet World Stats). This is partly because the cost of telecommunications in the kingdom is too expensive for most Swazis and because many Swazi people do not have digital media literacy skills (Mthembu 2012, 133). In May 2012 the Socialbakers website reported that there were 63 760 Facebook users in Swaziland, but this number is also increasing: the number grew by 16 080 in the six months preceding their report (Socialbakers 2012). Most of these users are young, possibly reflecting the fact that they have access through university and tertiary colleges, or in urban areas, through their schools. A total of 40 per cent of Facebook users (24 866 users) are 18–24-year-olds; 24 per cent are aged 25–34 and 10 per cent are 16–17. Male users in Swaziland comprise 58 per cent and females 42 per cent (Socialbakers 2012). Other social media such as Twitter are less popular (Mthembu 2012, 133).

The use of social media has been gaining momentum. Mthembu (2012, 133) reports that ordinary Swazis have found a public space in which they can discuss issues that the local media dare not highlight. Manqoba Nxumalo (2011a) reports that in the recent past more young people have been using the Internet and social media not just to interact, but also to influence opinion with a view to effecting change in Swaziland. Young people in particular are also using Facebook to voice their anger at the established ruling regime. Nxumalo (2011a) states that Facebook has become an alternative form of media for many people, and that a 'new community is being built via social media, where journalism as we know it is distorted'. He cites Facebook activist, Mandla Ginindza, a member of the Facebook group April 12 Uprising, who wrote that people in Swaziland have been forced to rely on social media for information and for mobilising for change, because local newspapers have, in his view, failed to stand up to the repressive machinery of the state.

The freedom of expression afforded to people on Facebook is of concern to Swazi parliamentarians. As early as August 2010, the Minister of Information said the government was looking at possible laws to censor cyberspace (*Times of Swaziland*, 20 August 2011). In particular, there was concern that information about the Swazi royal family was being leaked to the wider world (*Times of Swaziland*, 22 March 2011). The Swaziland Prime Minister, Barnabas Dlamini, was concerned that Facebook stories were being reported in the mainstream media (*Times of Swaziland*, 3 February 2011). It had been reported that people in Swaziland were bypassing the 'official' media for Facebook, with a view to exposing the behaviour of the ruling elite. Swazi secret police intelligence officers were instructed to join Facebook in order to gain such information (*Times Sunday*, 3 February 2011).

For this present investigation, a study was made of social network sites in Swaziland that publish information that would not usually appear in the mainstream media. Examples include outright criticism of King Mswati III and the royal family; information about forthcoming events, protests and strikes which draw attention to the need for democratic reform in Swaziland; and commentary about the need for political change. A purposive set of social network sites was chosen for analysis and theoretical sampling was employed. This type of sampling selects a number of exemplary cases to help assess a particular phenomenon. There is no 'correct' number of cases – the researcher stops when it appears that sufficient examples of different manifestations of a phenomenon have been collected (Altheide in Wall 2005, 159).

Social media sites on Facebook, blogging sites and news groups were explored. Some social media activists use more than one platform to share their material. For example, the Swaziland Solidarity Network has two Google groups and one Facebook site. Swazi Media Commentary has two blog sites, two Facebook sites and a Twitter feed. Where this was the case, all platforms were included in the survey. Postings on Swazi Media Commentary are also further distributed by the AllAfrica.com news aggregator, which makes material available to websites across the world, but the number of posts distributed in this way was not counted. Table 1 lists the main social media sites offering space for types of material, information, analysis or commentary that would not normally be published in mainstream media within Swaziland. In all cases the sites described themselves in some way as disseminating information and/or commentary advocating change in Swaziland.

There were many similarities between the various sites in terms of content, for example, all included official statements published verbatim from organisations with agendas to replace the existing political system in Swaziland. Among these organisations were the Swaziland Solidarity Network, Swaziland United Democratic Front, Swaziland Diaspora Platform, Swaziland Communist Party and the People's United Democratic Party.

The sites also included links to items in the mainstream media outside of Swaziland, most often South Africa, including reports or journalistic commentary about events pertaining to Swaziland. These included reports critical of King Mswati and the royal family, or about the deteriorating economic situation in the kingdom and its disproportionate effect on poorer members of the community.

There were also links to items published on the *Times of Swaziland* or *Swazi Observer* websites that contained information about pro-democracy activities in Swaziland, such as protest marches, the delivery of petitions to government ministries, and strikes. The sites also contain original material, including information about forthcoming events, meetings or marches, or about the conduct of state forces during protest activities in Swaziland, such as police arresting protest leaders. Among the original material were commentaries and analyses on matters relating to human rights/pro-democracy issues in Swaziland.

Membership statistics are as at 30 May 2012. It is important to remember that member-ship statistics are only one indicator of a site's popularity. It is not necessary to be a member to be able to access and read the sites; it is only a requirement for those wishing to post. In addition to those listed in Table 1, there were a number of other Facebook sites that did not describe themselves specifically as seeking change in Swaziland, but that nonetheless contained material that was generally supportive of change. Sites included the Swaziland National Association of Teachers, the Trade Union Congress of Swaziland and the Swaziland Youth in Action. Common characteristics of the listed social media sites include the sites' origins, the content of the material posted, and the identities of those making the posts.

Table 1: Social media sites offering a view on Swaziland not usually afforded by mainstream media

Facebook

Name	No. of members	url
April 12 Swazi Uprising	4 500	https://www.facebook.com/groups/shisa.mlilo/members/
My New Democratic Swaziland	115	https://www.facebook.com/groups/120232791385226/members/
Swaziland Democracy Campaign	412	https://www.facebook.com/groups/129594823639/members/
Swazi Media Commentary / Richard Rooney (two sites with identical information)	958 (total of both sites)	https://www.facebook.com/groups/142383985790674/members/
Swaziland National Union of Students	607	https://www.facebook.com/groups/439930195696/
Swaziland Solidarity Network Forum	2 837	https://www.facebook.com/groups/301238832249/members/
Umgosi Eswantini (The Real Staff) The Return	5 655	https://www.facebook.com/groups/183294745046213/members/

Google Group

Name	No of members	url
Swaziland Solidarity Network	801	http://groups.google.com/group/sa-swaziland-solidarity-eom-forum

Blogs

Name	url
Swaziland Diaspora Platform	http://swazidiaspora.blogspot.com
Swazi Media Commentary / Swaziland Commentary (two sites with identical information)	www.swazimedia.blogspot.com

None of the sites are run full-time in opposition to the mainstream media in Swaziland. All of them appear to have relatively small, but seemingly highly committed, participants as originators and/or readers. As far as can be ascertained, many of the sites are based outside of Swaziland, but within southern Africa. The most active sites, the Swaziland Solidarity Network (SSN), the Swaziland Diaspora, and the Swaziland Democracy Campaign, are based in South Africa. Swazi Media Commentary began life in Swaziland and presently comes from Botswana. The April 12 Uprising, Umgosi Eswatini (The Real Staff) and Swaziland National Union of Students seem to be based inside Swaziland. It is not clear where My New Democratic Swaziland is based.

Although there are a growing number of sites and a growing number of friends or group members, the number of people making posts is relatively small. For example, posting to Swaziland Solidarity Network site, which has 2 837 members, is confined to a small number of activists; probably no more than a dozen people could be counted as regular posters of original content. The number of people commenting on posts is larger, but no more than 50. The amount of traffic – postings – can vary according to circumstances. During times of political activity, for example a strike or mass demonstration, traffic rises to several posts a day. At other times, traffic might be slower, for example, from 5 to 11 June 2012, of the two most frequently updated Facebook sites, SSN, had 20 new posts and Swazi Media Commentary had 13. This was during a period of little political activity in Swaziland. By contrast, from 11–14 April 2011, a period of mass demonstrations in Swaziland, the Swazi Media Commentary blogsite had a total of 92 posts. It is impossible to verify traffic on SSN for this period.

A further characteristic of the sites is the multi-posting of the same material to a number of different sites. For example, material on the SSN site is dominated by that posted by the SSN official spokesperson, and includes original official statements of the organisation (written by the spokesperson) or material linked from other sites, notably mainstream media sites, which he identifies as being relevant to the aims of the organisation. In this way it is possible to see an SSN statement reproduced on a large number of pro-democracy social media sites, thereby giving it a larger reach than from its own site alone.

When asking to what extent the social media have been an empowering force in Swaziland, it is clear that social media sites have extended the public sphere to offer opportunities for a wider range of people both in the country and outside it, to produce, distribute and exchange information and commentary about the kingdom – especially in the context of the need for political change. People speak in their own voices and are not mediated in the way mainstream media are in Swaziland. However, even as more opportunities are made available, so barriers to participation exist, because of the inequalities of access to digital media technologies and unequal capacities to participate in a digital public sphere.

The use of social media disregards traditional gatekeeping models of journalism in Swaziland, where news-gathering is highly controlled and authority is exclusively held by professional journalists. The users of social media also become participants in news-making processes. Mthembu (2012, 133) identifies a 'constant sourcing' of story ideas, by newspapers, from social networks – Facebook in particular. Motsamai (2011, 47) reports that in Swaziland the pro-democracy movement is largely organised and held together by online networks. She adds that there are limits to how this aids the potential growth of the movement, since the nature of networked activism may further entrench the urban–rural political and cultural divide.

There is little evidence that social media sites are capable of becoming vehicles for actual change in Swaziland. To explore this further, a case study is offered of one Facebook site, the April 12 Uprising group, which had clearly-stated objectives to encourage an uprising in the kingdom and set a date for the intended action to take place.

The group emerged in early 2011 following the Arab Spring (uprisings in Northern Africa and the Middle East) in which Facebook and Twitter were reported to have played a significant part in mobilising people (Ghannam 2011).

On its Facebook site, the group stated its aim as follows:

> We pledge, as a group, to create in the next few months the biggest mass movement that the country has ever seen. 2011 will also mark the year when we will topple the royalist regime. Joining this group is a pledge that you will work tirelessly to make this a reality. The date set for our uprising is April 12 2011, the day which marks 38 years of servitude and powerlessness for Swaziland's toiling masses.

The group modelled itself on Facebook groupings which arose during the so-called Arab Spring, in countries such as Tunisia, Egypt, Bahrain and Oman (WordPress 2011). According to Nxumalo (2011b), the Swazi April 12 Uprising 'provided a platform for democracy activists to reorganise and share ideas about the prospects for change in Swaziland'. The Facebook group spoke to a new generation of youth that was more militant and angry, and became a platform for people from all walks of life and different political inclinations to discuss the problems in their country. But the uprising itself failed to materialise, partly because not enough of the masses cared to be mobilised by the Facebook agitators and partly because Swaziland's security forces took preemptive action against the leaders. On the day of the intended uprising, the Swazi police and defense forces arrested upwards of 150 leaders of the pro-democracy movement (Freedom House 2011b).

It may be that the leaders of the planned uprising were naïve to announce in advance the date of their action, thereby giving state forces ample opportunity to prepare. Peter Kenworthy (2011), however, concludes that the Facebook activity might have generated unrealistic excitement and anticipation on the part of the general population who became mere spectators, while the bulk of those who had generated the Facebook hype resided outside the country and could not coordinate activities on the ground to actuate their cyber aspirations.

Dimpho Motsamai (2011, 44) is probably right in saying that the April 12 Uprising failed because other factors, necessary for a revolution to succeed, were absent in Swaziland. Among such conditions are that the regime must appear irremediably unjust or inept, and must be viewed as a threat to the country's future, and that the political elite should be alienated from the state to the extent that they are no longer willing to defend it. In addition, broad-based mobilisation across socio-economic classes must follow; and international powers must either refuse to step in to defend the government or prevent it from using maximum force to defend itself.

References

Freedom House. 2011a. Swaziland 2011. Washington: Freedom House. http://old.freedomhouse.org/template.cfm?page=251&country=8140&year=2011 (accessed 31 May 2012).

Freedom House. 2011b. Government of Swaziland must engage with democratic movement. Washington: Freedom House. http://www.freedomhouse.org/article/government-swaziland-must-engage-democratic-movement (accessed 31 May 2012).

Ghannam, J. 2011. Social media in the Arab world: Leading up to the uprisings of 2011. Washington: Center for International Media Assistance.

Internet World Stats. 2012. Africa Internet Facebook usage and population statistics. www.internetworldstats.com/africa.htm#sz (accessed 31 May 2012).

Kenworthy, P. 2011. Swaziland: Uprising in the slip-stream of North Africa. *Pambazuka News*, 29 June. http://www.pambazuka.org/en/category/features/74436 (accessed 31 May 2012).

Motsamai, D. 2011. Swaziland: Can southern Africa democratise? *African Security Review* 20(2): 42–50. http://dx.doi.org/10.1080/10246029.2011.594301

Mthembu, M. 2012. National overview 2011, Swaziland. In *So this is democracy?* MISA: Windhoek. http://www.misa.org/researchandpublication/democracy/democracy.html (accessed 31 May 2012).

Nxumalo, M. 2011a. Swaziland: The fall of the orthodox, and the rise of social media. *Free Africa Media*, 24 February. http://freeafricanmedia.com/opinionista/2011-02-24-swaziland-the-fall-of-the-orthodox-and-the-rise-of-social-media (accessed 31 May 2012).

Nxumalo, M. 2011b. Swaziland: Time for honest reflection on April 12 Uprising. *Daily Maverick*, 15 April 2011. http://dailymaverick.co.za/article/2011-04-15-swaziland-time-for-honest-reflection-on-april-12-uprising (accessed 31 May 2012).

Socialbakers. 2012. Swaziland Facebook statistics. http://www.socialbakers.com/facebook-statistics/swaziland (accessed 28 May 2012).

US State Department. 2011. 2010 Human rights report: Swaziland, Bureau of Democracy, Human Rights, and Labor. http://www.state.gov/j/drl/rls/hrrpt/2010/af/154372.htm (accessed 31 May 2012).

Wall, M. 2005. Blogs of war. *Weblogs as News in Journalism* 6(2): 153–172. DOI: 10.1177/1464884905051006

WordPress. 2011. Swazi uprising: The exclusive WordPress interview. http://swaziapril12zing.wordpress.com/2011/03/07/swazi-uprising-the-exclusive-interview/ (accessed 31 May 2012).

Participatory journalism in Mozambique

Chris Paterson and Simone Doctors

This small case study addresses the phenomenon of participatory, non-professional and non-commercial informational communications in Mozambique, where, during social unrest in 2008, a popular blog – which is not primarily journalistic in nature – was alimented with eye-witness reporting by mobile phone calls and SMS (text messages) from a network of citizen journalists throughout the country. The blog – *Diário de um sociólogo* [Diary of a Sociologist] – was the best (indeed, in many cases the only) available source of information about the protests and the violent state response to them, whereas established local and international media provided little coverage and tended to offer reporting deeply influenced by the official accounts (which had an interest in minimising and ridiculing protests instigated by government policies). This research expands on the experience of one of the authors as a user, while resident in Maputo, of that blog.

Historical background

Portuguese rule in the country ended in 1975, and the former liberation movement (Frelimo) formed the first government of an independent Mozambique under the presidency of Samora Moises Machel. Soon after liberation, the country was plunged into a 17-year-long Cold War/proxy civil war, which thwarted the construction of a functional independent state. By the end of the conflict in 1992, the country's infrastructure was in ruins; despite the best attempts of the government and of a concerted international solidarity effort, the institutions, health and education systems of the new nation remained severely challenged, and Mozambique was ranked as the poorest country in the world.

Since 1994, there have been four national elections, all deemed free and fair to various extents by international observers and all won by Frelimo. Following a massive international aid effort, associated with often draconian internationally imposed structural reforms which were accepted by the government, Mozambique today has become the darling of the international development industry, a beacon of neoliberalism, with impressive rates of growth as measured by the average GDP. But this apparent success story hides a very different reality for the average Mozambican citizen: around 50 per cent of the population is unemployed, while many of those who have work earn salaries which do not cover their basic needs, as the prices of food, fuel and transport continue to rise in line with global trends. There is a perception in many quarters that the ruling class – buoyed up on international aid and pursuing their own interests with apparent impunity, while paying only lip service to the need for good governance and respect for human rights – has lost touch with these realities (see the critical review of Mozambican structural reform by Jones [2005], for example).

Mainstream and new media journalism in Mozambique

It is useful to review the state of mainstream news media in Mozambique in the post-war period, in order to place emerging alternative systems of journalism into context. Gaster (2011) observes that 'Mozambique's first multiparty Constitution of 1990 and its 2004 revision guarantee freedom of expression, association and the press. They also explicitly state that the "exercise of freedom of expression [...] and the exercise of the right to information shall not be limited by censorship"'. However, Salgado (2012, 1) writes that although 'the media environment in Mozambique is considered fairly liberal or partly free ... low wages and the lack of adequate journalistic training leave journalists vulnerable to bribes, intimidation and pressure. Government crackdowns on journalists engender a widespread practice of self-censorship, particularly in political issues.' The mainstream media are dominated by the *Notícias* newpaper – which is closely tied to the ruling party – and the state broadcasters (TVM, *Rádio Moçambique*), although two small commercial television broadcasters, STV and TIM, seem to have grown increasingly influential in the past few years. The newspaper *Savana* has long played a key role as an independent voice (Kasoma 1995), and a weekly free newspaper, *Verdade*, which appears in print and online, often provides an alternative to *Notícias*.

The development of Mozambican journalism in the post-independence period is described comprehensively by Fauvet and Mosse in their 2003 biography of the journalist Carlos Cardoso, who was assassinated in 2000. From the early 1990s, Cardoso, with other journalists, founded a number of independent reporting projects (*Mediacoop, Mediafax, Metical, Savana*) to provide news to Mozambicans from outside of dominant governmental and party structures. Coming well before widespread Internet use and availability, Mediafax arrived to subscribers by fax, and so was free of production and printing costs. The service has been widely lauded as an especially innovative means of maintaining investigative, watchdog journalism in the face of powerful institutions which had little taste for it.

While the majority of presses and broadcasters in Mozambique were reserved in their challenges to government and the structural violence of neoliberal reform in the 2000s, Salgado (2012) observes that a vibrant critical blogosphere emerged. Some blogs have been anonymous, some authored by named journalists, and many – including the one examined here – published by academics. During the same period, as in the rest of Africa, mobile phone use increased dramatically. Gaster (2011) provides a useful and contemporary summary of information and communication technology (ICT) access in Mozambique:

> Internet access is available via broadband, wireless or mobile phone in Maputo and all ten provincial capitals, and an increasing number of towns in the country's 128 districts. As in other African countries, more and more citizens are turning to the two mobile phone networks (MCel and Vodacom) for internet access, in addition to voice and SMS use, as mobile internet access is more widely available, cheaper and often more reliable. Around six million of Mozambique's 20 million inhabitants now own mobile phones.

Diário de um sociólogo

This case study focuses on the blog *Diário de um sociólogo*,[1] published by Carlos Serra since April 2006. Serra is a sociologist based at the Centro de Estudos Africanos at the Universidade Eduardo Mondlane (UEM) in Maputo, Mozambique. The blog contains the author's reflections on sociological and political life in Mozambique, supplemented by his posts of articles, stories, reports, posters, photos, cartoons and images from online newspapers and other electronic sources (*O País* online; *Savana*; *Domingo*). The early entries post few comments from readers, although there are a few 'flurries of activity' around certain entries: for example, 14 comments to an open letter to the president about the illegal export from Mozambique of natural resources on 30 January 2007. Then the blog gradually gained popularity (as documented by records of hits connected with each monthly blog archive page) and was named 'most read Mozambican blog' for 2007, with 272 daily visits and an average of 844 pages consulted daily, according to Site Meter records linked to the blog. During the social unrest of May 2008, the number of visits to the blog exploded, as it became a widely recognised source of information about what was happening in Maputo and elsewhere.

Sources tend to agree that protest and violence in the streets of Maputo and other Mozambican cities in early May 2008 stemmed from public anger at sudden (state-sanctioned) rises in food and transport prices. But sources reporting these protests at the time differ strikingly in their characterisation of events. Four distinct forms of journalism which emerged during the period of political unrest in 2008, are identified here: blogging, non-state media, state media and international media.

The Serra blog

During the food and fuel riots of 5 February 2008, the blog changes from a repository of sociological reflections and analyses, and begins to play the role of a communications hub. Serra himself echoed the experiences of many who had lived through the events when he commented some months later that it was 'the first, often the only, but always the most detailed and in-depth source of information and analysis of 5 February, with dozens of daily entries and updates' (Diário, 31 December 2008).[2]

The first entry on 5 February 2008 stated that there seemed to be a popular revolt in certain areas of Maputo, following hikes in the price of bread and *chapa* (private collective mini-bus) fares, which had come into effect that morning. Serra posted that he had been informed by fellow citizens that *chapa*s had stopped running in certain zones and barricades had been erected. One update reported that a car with armed police had been seen driving towards the quarter of Malhazine. Throughout the day Serra updated the blog 51 times between 10:00 and 22:21.

On the basis of information provided to him by SMS, calls from mobile phones or via email from informants all over the city, he posted the unfolding of the riots, as progressively more streets were barricaded, tyres burned, cars damaged and bonfires lit. He posted comments from informants identified either anonymously – as 'citizens I spoke to' (or similar) or, more specifically, as 'journalists', 'a psychologist', or 'one of my assistants' – or by name: the sociologist Carlos Bravo informed him of 'scenes of vandalism', shots being fired in the zones of Xiquelene, Hulene and Mavalane, and the 'involvement of young people who are minors'. It is noteworthy that Serra identifies many of those contributing information to the blog as 'journalists', implying they are professional journalists from various Mozambican media outlets (but this is not something the authors have been able to confirm). Serra also refers to media sources such as the BBC (presumably, BBC World Service) the Portuguese channel, STV (local commercial television), the online version of *O País* newspaper, *Rádio Moçambique* and Sapo.pt (a Portuguese portal).

After 11 addenda describing scenes of considerable violence and turbulence were posted over two hours, Serra implicitly signalled the lack of mainstream media coverage of these events in a post at 12:07, which read: '*Rádio Moçambique* is transmitting news of the football Cup of Nations which is taking place in Ghana.' His addendum of 12:32 stated that *Rádio Moçambique* had begun the 12:30 newsflash with the news that in certain quarters of the city there had been agitations due to the 'alleged' increase in *chapa* fares. Throughout the day the blog continued to publish news sent in by individuals located across the city, or gleaned by Serra from other media sources: the BBC, STV, *Rádio Moçambique* and Sapo.pt (which appears to provide limited news coverage of Lusophone Africa). Serra reported that he was interviewed by both the BBC Portuguese language service and STV, suggesting that these media regarded him as among the best informed sources on the day.

During this long day of reporting, Serra provided frequent updates on the blog, with detailed eyewitness accounts. At times he would insert, as breaking news, his own observations; for example, that local mobile phone services were becoming congested. The reporting during this day was very much in the classic telegraphic tone of a neutral reporter passing on information at a time of crisis, and all comment on the possible causes of the events being reported is well removed in the blog from these reports (coming some time later).

Local media: State and non-state

As noted above, Mozambique has an established and fairly vibrant non-state media sector, with some media being commercial, and others not. While not a focus of this study, there are reports that these provided critical reporting and analyses of the events, and – in the case of Maputo television broadcaster STV – some collaboration with

Serra. But the coverage of the event by the official media reflected the official tone. The protagonists were described as 'popular and opportunistic elements demonstrating in a violent manner', 'people of questionable conduct and children emotionally caught up to participate in acts of vandalism' and 'small armies of the unemployed and people of questionable conduct' (*Notícias*, 6 February 2008). In the official media, the events which triggered the riots (a 50 per cent rise in *chapa* fares and a significant rise in the price of bread) were evoked in the most neutral of terms, with no mention of the human context or implications of such increases in a context of extreme poverty, where ordinary people are already in dire straits. The tone was generally moralistic, neutral and dispassionate, evoking the unfortunate consequences of the riots (funerals being postponed, education disrupted, etc.) with no mention of the human reality behind them.

International media

On 5 February 2008, the Portuguese-language page of the BBC World Service published a short account of the events, directly based on the article which appeared the same day in *O Pais* online. It appears the international BBC Online reported twice on the events, in brief stories which depended heavily on official sources and provided no evidence of original reporting from the scene. On 6 February, five days after the worst of the riots, BBC Online reported the Mozambican government's statement that it would suspend the planned transport price increases. BBC Online noted that 'a person was killed by police in riots ... More than 60 people were also wounded when officers opened fire on the protesters.' An update of the story followed on 13 February, reporting 'clashes between police and rioters that killed at least four people and seriously injured more than 100'. The central body of the short article conveyed the government's position, and referred to the protests only in terms of the damage to property: 'During the demonstrations, crowds looted shops, destroyed vehicles and burned tyres and electricity poles' – the same theme dominating coverage of the story in the official local media. However, one person is quoted at the end of the story as saying: 'The key problem is people's low salary' and suggesting that protest was reasonable.

The authors examined news agency reports from *Deutsche Presse-Agentur* (DPA), Reuters, and *Agence France-Presse* (AFP). Over the course of the next week there were additional reports from these international news agencies, some tied to outbreaks of further violence, but all appearing to rely almost exclusively on Mozambican state radio, and several relying on one city mayor quoted there. They all emphasised the damage to property and offered little explanation to international media of what had instigated protests on such a scale. The explanation of deaths earlier in the week followed the government position that 'police opened fire on stone-throwing protestors'. A Reuters report on 12 February added the additional detail that 'thousands of protesters' were involved, but only in the context of those protesters having 'clashed with police'. The story which (given that Reuters is the main source for African news for English-language media worldwide) would have been widely used internationally, provides as its main quote the same mayor remarking: 'We called them (the protesters) for a dialogue, but nobody accepted our offer, making it difficult for us to understand the real motives of the violent demonstration.' Only later in the Reuters story is it mentioned that the Mozambican government had proposed 'a 50-percent rise in mass transport fares' and 'the bulk of its 20 million people continue to eke out a subsistence living and many are mired in poverty'.

Conclusions

In summary, the story was reported to Mozambicans through four overlapping journalistic forms:

- Blogging provided immediacy, detail, eye-witness reporting and a critique of the causes of the rioting and the violent police response. Some of this reporting fed into the news coverage of non-state media, especially STV (commercial television);
- Non-state commercial media such as *Savana*, *O Pais* and STV provided similarly critical reporting and analysis, though with less immediacy;
- State-owned/influenced media provided no coverage initially, and then only official interpretations demonising protesters;
- Foreign media (including news agencies) provided almost no detail or context, and depended on the accounts of officials relayed via state media, which described the protests as irrational and unprovoked (whereas they were provoked by sudden, government-condoned rises in the price of transport and bread, which the majority of people could not afford), and minimised state violence against the protesters.

In February 2008, the Serra blog provided an early and unusual case of crowd-sourcing breaking news. A fast-developing crisis with significant political and public safety implications, across all social strata, was reported comprehensively and with immediacy, over a broad geographic area, with considerable independence from dominant institutional forces, and, almost exclusively, by a highly informal network of informants using mobile phones to inform a blogger. In short, the case represents an early triumph for participatory journalism. That the public protests were also, in no small part, instigated through the use of mobile phones as an informal political organising tool, speaks to the revolutionary potential of these technological developments across various realms of social life – potential which seems to be accentuated in the contexts of some African countries where communications opportunities had previously been highly constrained.

At the beginning of September 2010, widespread social unrest erupted once again in Mozambique following further price hikes. However, this time STV had live coverage of the events, showed live footage of the riots, and interviewed citizens and commentators. In this regard Gaster (2011) notes that 'independent television companies made an effort to provide real-time news'. Gaster (ibid.) reported that at least 13 people were killed during the protests, mostly (if not entirely) by poorly trained and poorly prepared police. In her account, Gaster credits Serra's blog as being one source of information about the 2010 events, along with the Facebook page of the free newspaper *Verdade*. In contrast to his highly eyewitness-sourced reporting of unrest as it occurred in 2008, in September 2010 Serra provided fewer updates and relied far more on media accounts. According to Gaster (pers. comm., 29 September 2012), the main explanation for this shift was that by 2010 Facebook had begun to displace blogs as the main forum for participatory journalism; there is the suggestion that during the 2010 riots Facebook fulfilled the function of informal news processor, taking over the role played by Serra's blog in 2008.[3] Indeed, as increasing numbers of users turn to Facebook, the 2008 riots may well have marked the zenith of blogging in Mozambique. Wasserman (2011, 157) concludes his overview of the role of mobile phones in facilitating social change in Africa with the suggestion that these technologies are allowing people on the continent to transgress 'hitherto fixed boundaries of what counts as political participation or civic identification'. This study has offered such an example from Lusophone Africa.

Notes

1 http://oficinadesociologia.blogspot.co.uk

2 The blog is entirely in Portuguese. All translations to English are by co-author Doctors, unless otherwise indicated.

3 See, for example, a comment sent to the blog of Keita (2010), by a Mozambican resident of Maputo who affirmed: 'Facebook played a very important role in disseminating accurate information about the riots … I knew exactly what was going on in 7 or 8 streets of Maputo … people turned to Facebook to know which road they should use to pick up their kids from school when the riots started or to return home safely.'

References

Atton C. and H. Mabweazara. 2011. New media and journalism practice in Africa: An agenda for research. *Journalism* (August) 12(6): 667–673.

Banda, F., O.F. Mudhai and W.J. Tettey. 2009. Introduction: New media and democracy in Africa – a critical interjection. In *African media and the digital public sphere*, ed. O.F. Mudhai, W.J. Tettey and F. Banda, 1–20. New York: Palgrave Macmillan.

Chichizola, J. 1995. Mediafax, the right number (originally *La Lettre Feb. 1994*, trans. H. Vivien-Neal). *Index on Censorship* 1: 192.

Fauvet, P. and M. Mosse. 2003. *Carlos Cardoso: Telling the truth in Mozambique.* Cape Town: Double Storey.

Gaster, P. 2011. Mozambique: ICTs and the September street protests in Maputo. *Global Information Society Watch*: 193–196. http://www.giswatch.org/en/country-report/social-mobilisation/mozambique (accessed 15 November 2012).

Jones, B.G. 2005. Globalisations, violences, and resistances in Mozambique. In *Critical theories, international relations, and 'the anti-globalisation movement': The politics of global resistance*, ed. C. Eschle and B. Maiquashca, 53–73. London: Routledge.

Keita, M. 2010. New media tools bring Mozambican crisis to the world. *Committee to Protect Journalists: CPJ Blog*, 3 September. http://cpj.org/blog/2010/09/new-media-brings-crisis-in-mozambique-to-the-world.php (accessed 15 November 2012).

Mudhai, O.F., W.J. Tettey and F. Banda, eds. 2009. *African media and the digital public sphere.* New York: Palgrave Macmillan.

Nyamnjoh, F. 2005. *Africa's media: Democracy & the politics of belonging.* London: Zed Books.

Salgado, S. 2012. The Web in African countries. *Information, Communication & Society* 15(9): 1–17.

Teer-Tomaselli, R. and T. Lima. 1996. Mediacoop Mozambique. *Agenda* 12(31): 54–55.

Wasserman, H. 2011. Mobile phones, popular media, and everyday African democracy: Transmissions and transgressions. *Popular Communication* 9(2): 146–158.

Social media and the politics of ethnicity in Zimbabwe

Shepherd Mpofu

The architecture of the Internet has, over the years, promised greater freedom of assembly and expression to different communities. New platforms have been created where people can imagine and debate identity, (re)create communities and share experiences (Mitra 2001; Moyo 2009; Ogola 2011). For suppressed communities like Zimbabweans in the diaspora and in their homeland, the Internet is the safest and most reliable platform (Moyo 2009) for effectively (re)producing competing notions of nationalism (Peel 2009) and identity from below (Khalidi 2010, xiii). Studies on the social media have proven the central role social media, in the form of dozens of diasporic Zimbabwean websites and radio stations, play as alternative sources of information and expression that serve both the diaspora and homeland populations (Mano and Willems 2006; Moyo 2007; Peel 2009).

Three opinion articles, published in 2008 on a Wales-based website (www.newzimbabwe.com), are analysed in this study. The contribution 'The Ndebele president', was written by Mduduzi Mathuthu, the website's editor. The second, 'Ndebele president: Minorities should not cease to dream', was penned by Itayi Garande, the then editor of a rival online publication based outside Zimbabwe, in response to Mathuthu's writings. The third piece, 'Ndebele president: The secret of fear', written by the Movement for Democratic Change (MDC) Deputy Secretary General, Priscilla Misihairambwi-Mushonga, argues that Zimbabwean politics is influenced by ethnicity. These contributions have deliberately been selected, as they are amenable to an analysis of ethnicity, as addressed here. In a case study conclusions made may not necessarily be universal, but they may be useful for the 'purpose of understanding a larger class of similar units (a population of cases)' (Gerring 2007, 37). The analysis of these articles and subsequent reader comments is based on critical discourse analysis (CDA), an 'explicitly normative analysis of how texts and discourses work in ideological interests with powerful political consequences' (Luke 2002, 96). In addition, this article looks at how 'dominance and inequality are enacted, reproduced, and resisted by text in the social and political context' (Wang 2010, 254).

Research in Zimbabwe (Mano and Willems 2008; Moyo 2007, 2009; Peel 2009) and elsewhere (Bernal 2006; Chan 2005; Laguerre 2005; Shuval 2000) reveals that new media play an important role by acting as 'connective tissue' among diasporeans, with some online activities culminating in social or political activities and opening up restricted democratic space, while resisting state propaganda. Newzimbabwe.com offers its readers a chance to be both consumers and producers of content – a development peculiar to online media. Whereas the public media are accused of being biased in their coverage of events (Nyahunzwi 2001; Waldahl 2004) and of systematically barring certain voices from being heard, the new media offer those who are marginalised, ostracised and demonised counter-hegemonic voices (Bailey, et al. 2007, xii; Dahlberg 2007) and, along with those who perpetrate these exclusions, a platform to access and debate issues of common public interest.

Newzimbabwe.com, the leading and biggest website covering Zimbabwean issues, is regularly updated. In addition, it has served as a template for websites with a Zimbabwean focus, since it is one of the first Zimbabwean online publications to be established outside Zimbabwe, by Zimbabweans. The website averages around 20 000 hits per day.[1] Its professional layout, regularly updated content and variety of contributors easily set it apart from others. Newzimbabwe.com was launched in June 2003 by five former Zimbabwean journalists (Moyo 2007). It caters for the homeland as well as the burgeoning population of diaspora communities, which numbers anything between 3.4 and 4.5 million (Kanu 2010; Landau 2008; Terera 2008).

Ethnicity and national identity in Zimbabwe

Postcolonial Zimbabwe is under identity stress, mainly because the difficult process of nation-state formation went wrong from independence (Masunungure 2006; Ndlovu 2010). This was due to the misconceived notion that the liberation war automatically created a nation (Carr 2007) out of an ethnically diverse society characterised by the simmering 'danger of an outburst of tribal feeling' (Shamuyarira 1965, 185; Sithole 1980). This shows that ethnicity is not merely an empty marker of identity, but a value-laden political tool (Ake 1993) that influences political life in Zimbabwe.[2] Two years after the war of independence (1982–1987), the problem of ethnicity became apparent when ZANU-PF delivered Zimbabwe into a civil war that left over 20 000 dead (CCJP 1999). This was in response to unconfirmed claims that PF-ZAPU (ZANU-PF's rival in nationalist politics) had arms caches on its farms in the Midlands and Matabeleland regions – its strongholds – and was preparing for war. This 'civil war' genocide, code-named *Gukurahundi* (a Shona word meaning 'the early rain that washes away the chaff before the spring rains'), was executed by the Shona-speaking North-Korean-trained Fifth Brigade military outfit (Todd 2007). The episode, which Mugabe later labelled a 'moment of madness', still influences identity debates in Zimbabwe, since it 'not only left deep scars among the victims but also intensified Matabeleland regionalism' (Muzondidya 2009, 177) and particularism. This state of affairs is partly informed by the elite 'pact of forgetting', made in 1987, when Nkomo (the PF-ZAPU leader) and Mugabe (the ZANU-PF leader) signed a unity accord.

New media and taboo issues: Online media and discursive constructions of identity

Mathuthu's provocative contribution observes that ethnicity has informed state power control since independence. Itayi Garande (2008) dismisses this notion, arguing: 'I do not think that tribalism persists as an active contemporary phenomenon that can be used to provide a sound narrative of mainstream and contemporary Zimbabwean politics.' Garande also dismisses historical and current ethnic tensions in Zimbabwean politics as a way of understanding the current political dynamics. Priscilla Misihairambwi-Mushonga's contribution, 'Ndebele President: The secret of fear' deals with contemporary Zimbabwean politics from the perspective of an opposition party politician. She argues (2008) that Zimbabwean politics 'is nothing but disguised tribalism' and discussing these issues in the public media is taboo.

Taboo, in this context, are voices on issues that the ruling elite have silenced or criminalised, and therefore cannot be discussed within Zimbabwe as they are likely to cause 'division' among citizens. The social media, however, have opened avenues for such discussions. Readers are provoked to engage with Mathuthu's writings in different ways. A reader, Sophie Zvapera,[3] comments that 'this is an important soul searching topic ... ' and Sibanda adds that 'the issue you raised should be supported ...' Gomo Douglas comments: 'I am a regular visitor of the [your] newspaper. I must congratulate you for writing such an inspired and well thought out piece of work ... ' Special One reacts by saying: 'firstly i would like to say to mathuthu dream on and never in a million years will there be an Ndebele president in Zimbabwe. Obama did not win because of tribe, but mainly because of race which makes it totally a different case ... '

Some readers view the initiative to confront ethnicity as a key ingredient to political power and state control as divisive. Madhobha, for instance, asks: 'Ndebele president *kuita sei* (translated from Shona: what for)? Its people like you, who are in a position of power, i mean media who continue to divide the country.' Another argument from the readers is that substance, not ethnicity, matters in the configuration of state power.

State power, ethnicity and national identity

Media institutions help reproduce social norms, behaviours and stereotypes that naturalise society's values and beliefs. The argument here is that the internet can also purvey certain myths and beliefs. Sophie Zvapera summarily captures a widely circulated political myth that

> the political landscape in Zimbabwe is so tribally defined that in all political formations all that Ndebeles are rewarded with is a Deputy ... position ... If a Ndebele seeks leadership beyond ... [that] they are ostracized. The genocide ... was a clear message that Ndebeles should never challenge a Shona leader and they have continue to pay with lack of development and denial of access to the national cake ....

In a comment suggesting the impossibility of occupying political power based on merit, JJ argues that there are broader advantages to being Shona, as 'people of non-Shona heritage who have had to carry the cross of being born of non-Shona heritage and this

117

has curtailed their opportunities in life within Zimbabwe'.[4] Vulindlela adds: 'If you look at many countries in Africa ... you will realise that tribes have determined the presidency – its not about performance, effectiveness, intelligence, vision or anything.' The argument here is that ethnicity influences political choices.

Another common myth among some contributors, and in Zimbabwe in general, is that the Ndebele are meant to be deputies, not leaders. This is expressed by Nicol, commenting on Misihairambwi-Mushonga's article: 'why are you fighting for a ndebele president when even the ndebeles know that the only position they can occupy is deputy'.[5]

While some readers believe ethnicity is a qualification for political power, others believe holding presidential office must be based on merit. Nehokera11 states that Ndebele and Shona are the same: 'any one of us ... must have the right to contest for the highest office ... ' Butho Ndlela adds: 'It's not about a Ndebele State or Shona State ... its about the republic of Zimbabwe' and finally Smiler Mucaradi argues that '[t]he issue is not Ndebele or Shona. The issue is being intelligent. Anyone can be President in Zimbabwe as long as they appear to be mobilising the entire country or the greater part of the country.'

Mythologies of belonging

Another myth circulated in national identity debates in Zimbabwe is that Shonas primordially belong to Zimbabwe, while Ndebeles migrated from South Africa. Counter-myths argue that Shonas do not belong as they migrated from up north. Most comments suggest that Ndebeles violently occupied the country from the south, as alluded to by Jonah Moyo's statement: 'Ndeveres [derogatory term for Ndebeles] are not Zimbabweans as they say, everytime you see a Ndebele out of zim they say we are southafricans so why do they need to lead a foreign country.' Under Mathuthu's article, Josh Mhambi asserts that 'there is also the issue of Ndebele's being foreigners ... We may not want to trace the genesis of our neighbours in the country [Shonas] ... they have a lot to lose.' Amasalad24, commenting under Misihairambwi-Mushonga's article, opines that 'you were lucky that we didn't throw you out back to your South Africa. Forget ... no Ndebele will be a leader, Zimbabwe will never be yours.' Zvinoita_Chete advances an idea which is mostly promoted by nationalists, namely that both Ndebeles and Shonas 'basically come from the same mothers' and therefore 'ndebele [and] shona same same' (*Zim* 2008). These sentiments show the fluidity and the constructed nature of identity (Wilson 2000).

Genocide memory and identity

Gukurahundi memory is integral to understanding the explosive nature of Zimbabwean ethno-politics, as it forms the core of most debates under the stories. From the narratives on *newzimbabwe.com*, suggestions abound that there must be conditions for a Ndebele to become president. These include a promise not to avenge the *Gukurahundi*, which is informed by the myth that Shonas killed Ndebeles, thus insinuating that all Shonas were the perpetrators. Genocide memory, which is a mainstay in the consciousness of most online discussants, is used to define Zimbabwean-ness (Castells 2004). An incisive comment from *ndumiso ncube* shows that the genocide is key to ethic particularism, collective memory and ethnic cohesion: '[T]he Kukurahundi [Gukurahundi – SM] did not scare us infact it brought us very close to Zapu and Umdalawethu [our old man-Joshua Nkomo – SM]'.

The post-genocide feeling among Ndebeles is that of exclusion and bitterness, owing to the fact that no apology was made by Robert Mugabe. The discussants' suggestions point to the need for a truth and reconciliation commission, where people can account for their actions and attain closure. Andrew sibanda captures this:

> Think about the truth and reconciliation in south africa, atleast people talked about it and thats what we need in zim to heal the wounds of those that lost their loved ... The fact that we still view each other as shona and ndebele not zimbabweans show that our leaders have failed ... to unite zimbabweans and therefore there is noway [of] a ndebele president ....

David T Hwangwa is 'not of the belief [we will] have a Ndebele president overnight unless they promise the nation that there wont be attempts towards reversing and revenging what happened in the past'. The two comments confirm that Ndebeles as an ethnic group collectively identify with and use their genocide memory to make sense of their political existence in Zimbabwe. For instance, the exclusion of this ethnic group from the history narratives and state control is intimately linked with the genocide.

Conclusion

The argument made here is that social media have enabled expressions of both popular and unpopular constructions of identity and belonging, in a fashion unimaginable in public media. This places the new media on a pedestal of a liberating alternative public sphere, where dominant acts of silencing debates, deemed 'divisive' by authorities, are challenged. Contradictions among participants show a clear departure from the ZANU-PF imaginings of a cohesive nation-state and the centrality of debate in a democratic society. ZANU-PF imagined citizenship to be consolidated when the unity accord was signed between Nkomo and Mugabe, but Eric Worby (1998, 566) argues that the genocide period 'permanently stained the supposedly uniform cloth of post-colonial citizenship'. This stain continues to be a point of reference for both Shonas and Ndebeles in defining the nation-state's power to insiders and outsiders. This is informed by the Zimbabwean government's failure to adequately address the issue. The closest it came was with the formation of the misnamed Ministry of National Healing, whose minister was arrested in 2011 for attending a *Gukurahundi* memorial. Although such disagreements do not aid in constructing a cohesive national identity, they incubate the possibility of finding a democratic way to address the ethnic problem in Zimbabwe through open talk. One shortcoming of this study is that it has not discussed power relations in, and the political economy of, the Internet – due to limited space. Suffice to say that it has attempted to position a social medium as central counter-hegemonic platform for identity construction in authoritarian regimes.

Acknowledgement

The author would like to thank the Faculty of Humanities' SPARC Programme for funding, and Prof. Eric Worby and Dr Thabisani Ndlovu for their advice on the initial drafts of this article.

Notes

1   http://www.mediatico.com/en/goto.asp?url=10213

2   Zimbabwe has two main ethnic groups, the majority of Zimbabwe population, Shonas, at 76 per cent, while Ndebeles account for 20 per cent. Within these main groups are sub-ethnic groups which are not necessarily cohesive and homogeneous.

3   Names of readers are quoted as supplied by the people who posted comments. Their statements are reproduced as they appear on the website, with spelling, grammar and abbreviations unchanged. Where explanations are in order these are added for the sake of clarity.

4   http://www.newzimbabwe.com/opinion/opinion.aspx?newsid=4010

5   http://www.newzimbabwe.com/opinion/opinion.aspx?newsid=4010

References

Ake, C. 1993. What is the problem of ethnicity in Africa? *Transformation* 22: 1–14.

Burr, V. 2003. *Social constructionism*, 2nd edition. Essex: Routledge.

Castells, M. 2004. *The power of identity: The information age, economy, society and culture*, 2nd edition. Oxford: Blackwell.

Catholic Commission for Justice and Peace (CCJP). 1999. *Breaking the silence, building true peace: A report on the disturbances in Matabeleland and the Midlands, 1980–1988*. Harare: CCJP.

Chan, B. 2005. Imagining the homeland: The Internet and diasporic discourse of nationalism. *Journal of Communication Inquiry* 29(4): 336–368.

Garande, I. 2008. Ndebele president: Minorities should not cease to dream. http://www.newzimbabwe.com/pages/opinion351.19061.html (accessed 25 October 2011).

Gatsheni-Ndlovu, S. 2011. Dangers of myths to tribal relations in Zimbabwe. http://www.newzimbabwe.com/opinion-4902-Dangers%20of%20myths%20to%20tribal%20relations/opinion.aspx (accessed 27 October 2011).

Gerring, J. 2007. *Case study research: Principles and practices*. Cambridge: Cambridge University Press.

Kanu, J.M. 2010. Zimbabwe: Diaspora – untapped growth zone. http://allafrica.com/stories/201011250083.html (accessed 27 October 2011).

Landau, L. 2008. Drowning in numbers. In *Migration from Zimbabwe: Numbers, needs and policy options*, ed. S. Johnston, A. Bernstein and R. de Villiers, 19. Johannesburg: Centre for Development and Enterprise.

Luke, A. 2002. Beyond science and ideology critique: Developments in critical discourse analysis. *Annual Review of Applied Linguistics* 22: 96–110.

Mitra, A. 2001. Marginal voices in cyberspace. *New Media and Society* 3(1): 29–48.

Mano, W. and W. Willems. 2008. Emerging communities, emerging media: The case of a Zimbabwean nurse in the British *Big Brother* show. *Critical Arts* 22(1): 101–128.

Masunungure, E.V. 2006. Nation building, state building and power configuration in Zimbabwe. *Conflict Trends Magazine* 1: 1–10.

Mathuthu, M. 2008. The Ndebele president. http://www.newzimbabwe.com/blog/index.php/2008/11/mmathuthu/the-ndebele-president/ (accessed 25 October 2011).

Misihairambwi-Mushonga, P. 2008. Ndebele president: The secret of fear. http://www.newzimbabwe.com/opinion-4010-Ndebele%20president%20the%20secret%20fear/opinion.aspx (accessed 25 October 2011).

Moyo, D. 2007. Alternative media, diaspora and the mediation of the Zimbabwe crises. *Ecquid Novi: African Journalism Studies* 28(1/2): 81–105.

Moyo, L. 2009. Constructing a home away from home: Internet, nostalgia and identity politics among Zimbabwean communities in the diaspora. *Journal of Global Mass Communication* 2(1/2): 66–86.

Mugabe, R. 2003. Speech by His Excellency President Robert Gabriel Mugabe of Zimbabwe on the occasion of the World Summit on the Information Society, Geneva, Switzerland, 10 December 2003. http://www.itu.int/wsis/geneva/coverage/statements/zimbabwe/zw.pdf (accessed 25 October 2011).

Muzondidya, J. 2009. From buoyancy to crisis, 1980–1997. In *Becoming Zimbabwe: A history from the pre-colonial period to 2008*, ed. B. Raftopoulos and A. Mlambo, 167–200. Harare: Weaver Press.

Ndlovu-Gatsheni, S.J. 2009. *Do 'Zimbabweans' exist? Trajectories of nationalism, national identity formation and crisis in the post-colonial state.* Bern: Peter Lang.

Newzimbabwe.com. 2011. ZANU-PF must resolve Gukurahundi: Moyo. http://www.newzimbabwe.com/news-5814-Zanu%20PF%20must%20resolve%20Gukurahundi%20Moyo/news.aspx (accessed 28 October 2011).

Newzimbabwe.com. 2011, 15 April. Minister arrested over Gukurahundi memorial. http://www.newzimbabwe.com/news-4919-Gukurahundi%20minister%20arrested/news.aspx (accessed 27 October 2011).

Nyahunzvi, T.M. 2001. The Zimbabwe Mass Media Trust: An experiment that failed. *Media Development* 48(2): 31–36.

Peel, A.C. 2009. Diaspora ethnicity and politics in the electronic media: Case studies of United Kingdom-based Zimbabwean Internet websites and their associations. PhD thesis, University of Wales.

Potter, J. 1996. *Representing reality: Discourse, rhetoric and social construction.* London: Sage.

Shamuyarira, N. 1965. *Crisis in Rhodesia.* London: Andre Deutsch.

Shuval, J. 2000. Diaspora migration: Definitional ambiguities and a theoretical paradigm. *International Migration* 38(5): 41–57.

Sithole, M. 1980. Ethnicity and factionalism in Zimbabwe nationalist politics, 1957–79. *Ethnic and Racial Studies* 3(1): 17–39.

Takei, M. 1998. Collective memory as the key to national and ethnic identity: The case of Cambodia. *National and Ethnic Politics* 4(3): 59–78.

Terera, D. 2008. Perspectives on the brain drain. In *Migration from Zimbabwe: Numbers, needs and policy options*, ed. S. Johnston, A. Bernstein and R. de Villiers, 19–22. Johannesburg: Centre for Development and Enterprise.

Todd, J.G. 2007. *Through the darkness: A life in Zimbabwe.* Cape Town: Zebra Press.

Waldahl, R. 2004. *Politics and persuasion: Media coverage of Zimbabwe's 2000 election.* Harare: Weaver Press.

Wang, J. 2010. A critical discourse analysis of Barack Obama's speeches. *Journal of Language Teaching and Research* 1(3): 254.

Wilson, J.L. 2005. *Nostalgia: Sanctuary of meaning.* London: Routledge.

Worby, E. 1998. Tyranny, parody and ethnic polarity: Ritual engagements with the state in Northwestern Zimbabwe. *Journal of Southern African Studies* 24(3): 561–578.

'It's struck a chord we have never managed to strike': Frames, perspectives and remediation strategies in the international news coverage of *Kony2012*

Toussaint Nothias

The 2012 International Women's Day went rather unnoticed in most international media. At the time, the video *Kony2012*, by the American non-governmental organisation (NGO) Invisible Children (IC) went viral, eventually reaching 110 million hits (Chalk 2012, 3). Such a success for a 30-minute video was as surprising as the online reactions it spurred were violent and numerous. As international media covered this backlash, it further raised the video's profile. Yet, as Beckett (2012a, 6) points out, there was some confusion, on the side of the mainstream media, about how to report the story: 'Was this another "Gosh look what the Internet can do!" narrative? Or should they focus on the policy debate around the merits of campaigning for a United States (US)-backed military manhunt?' This short essay outlines the main frames used in various international media to report on *Kony2012*. It stresses the non-African portrayal of Africa on an unprecedented scale enabled by social media, while addressing the ways in which international journalists tried to remediate this. It also highlights the role of social media in including African voices in the coverage. Finally, it asks to what extent this event forced journalists to confront their past failings in reporting the Lord's Resistance Army (LRA) conflict.

Responding to the 'Kony-fication of their Facebook page', the Australian national network Ten broadcast *Kony2012* during a special programme (Rourke 2012). Similarly, France 24 dedicated most of its initial coverage to stress the unprecedented online 'buzz' (Dupuis 2012). Throughout the international media there was a shared sense of why the story was newsworthy: the viral success of a rather long video dealing with the dreadful actions of a violent Ugandan war criminal. Yet the tremendous notoriety gained by the video was instantly paralleled by strong criticisms – initially emerging from the blogs and posts of academics, journalists and development workers. Amidst the different criticisms, it became more complex for journalists to cover the story. *Kony2012* was not only a 'viral success', it had become an online debate which challenged the ethics and aesthetics of the video, its misleading nature, as well as its timing and the policies promoted by the campaign.

According to Chalk (2012, 5), the main criticism against the campaign was the policy advocated by IC. The video calls for US military intervention to help the Ugandan army track down Kony. Yet, as many stressed, promoting a military solution could have a dramatic, probably lethal, impact on those abducted and still held captive by the LRA. English photojournalist, Liz Wainright (in Curtis 2012), explained: 'It'll be children who are Kony's bodyguards. If they do get Kony there will be a wall of children to get through. How will they deal with that?' In fact, and as explained in the video, the US government had already agreed to send military advisors in Uganda. Hence, journalist Michael Wilkerson (2012), in a blog published on *Foreign Policy* – and subsequently quoted in mainstream media such as the BBC World Service – wondered: Is there a real threat that the forces already in place will be withdrawn, 'one that justifies such a massive production campaign and surely lucrative donation drive?' Other commentators took this criticism further by linking the video to US geopolitical interests in the region. Researcher Adam Branch (2012) argued on Al-Jazeera that *Kony2012* just made it easier for the US government to 'intervene militarily in a place rich in oil and other resources'.

Another widespread criticism in the international media was that the video misrepresented the current situation in Uganda. CNN Africa correspondent, David Mckenzie (2012), explained that 'it describes the situation in northern Uganda six years ago which bears no resemblance to the real life of people in Gulu'. Similarly, Ugandan journalist Rosebell Kagumire (2012) attacked this distortion of facts: 'It makes it sound as if Kony is still in Uganda. But Kony has left the country six years ago, this is simply not true.' This related to concerns that the video was detrimental to people in Uganda, because it did not address more pressing challenges. These include education, post-conflict rehabilitation and even a little-known condition possibly resulting from the war, nodding disease, which was brought to the attention of mainstream media by Ugandan journalist Angelo Izama (2012). In addition, the lack of historical contextualisation of the conflict and its simplification were also widely stressed, for instance by CNN chief international correspondent Christiane Amanpour (2012).

The contentious nature of Yoweri Museveni's government, as well as its past exactions, was also pointed out as blind spots in the video (Wilkerson 2012). France24 reporter, Aurore Dupuis (2012), quoted a blog on the *Independent* by Musa Okwonga, who complained about Museveni not being held accountable for the failure to catch Kony.[1] In this particular report, this was the only criticism made about the video, and, in a way, it implied that the Ugandan government was almost as 'bad' as Kony, without providing any further explanation or context. Without downplaying the criticism of Museveni, Dupuis' reporting also shows how easily international coverage can slip towards a form of Afro-pessimism. As such, it fed a pessimistic discourse about the ability of Ugandans to solve their own problems, while forgetting to acknowledge the most problematic aspects of the video, and in particular its colonial undertones.

As Becket (2012b) puts it, the simplistic narrative of the video 'reinforces the idea that the "West" (or just America, really) must "save" Africa where people are helpless victims of evil men' – a notion also known as the 'White man's burden'. The viewer is put in the position of Gavin, the son of Jason Russel, founder of IC. Jason, a young white American, tells the story of the promise he made to Jacob, a Ugandan teenager formerly abducted by the LRA, to catch Joseph Kony, the leader of the rebellion. Taken together, these characters epitomise three recurrent stereotypes that have pervaded Western representations of Africa: the good, willing Westerner, the helpless African and the cruel warlord. In doing so, it reproduces a binary colonial framework of black Africans as either 'child-like characters in need of help from the north, or as savage, wild and violent figures' (Orgeret 2010, 53). That such a colonial narrative – which stereotypes and disempowers Africans – was allowed to reach an unprecedented global audience through social media understandably was cause for concern – something many international media stressed.

Other criticisms – compiled promptly on the blog 'Visible Children' by a student in political science, Grant Oyston, which also went viral – condemned the narcissism of the video centred around Jason, the slick marketing, as well as the simple call for action appealing to an audience of apoliticised and apathetic young Americans (tweet celebrities, buy wristband and action kit, print colourful posters, and share the video on social media). These criticisms became part of the frame used by international media, and can in fact be understood as an attack of what Chouliaraki (2012) calls 'post-humanitarianism'. We are witnessing, she argues, changes in the ethics of solidarity in humanitarianism that are reflected in the changes of the aesthetics of humanitarian communication. At the heart of this post-humanitarianism lies a 'self-oriented morality, where doing good to others is about "how I feel" and must, therefore, be rewarded by minor gratification to the self' (Chouliaraki 2012, 3). This new ethics of solidarity – 'the celebration of a neoliberal lifestyle of "feel good altruism"' – is combined with a marketing logic of corporate world and online media, which then result in a new aesthetic of humanitarian communication (2012, 4). Although the video relied on tropes about Africa associated with more traditional humanitarian appeal, it also drew heavily on these three aspects of post-humanitarianism: it created a brand and manufactured goods 'StopKony'; it relied entirely on social media; it promoted the empowerment of its audience of donors much more than the one of suffering distant others.[2]

Given this post-humanitarian ethos and the reproduction of a colonial representation of Africa, the success of *Kony2012* raises questions about the ability of social media to foster a deep sense of global solidarity. However, the social media were also powerful in providing an immediate criticism of these aspects. In fact, while the video was rightfully criticised for not including any African voices – or any sense of local agency – the social media also allowed African voices to be heard in international coverage. Among others, Rosebell Kagumire and Angelo Izama, two Ugandan journalists, were interviewed or quoted on most international news organisations, including Al Jazeera, CNN, CNTV, the BBC, France24, the *LA Times*, *The New York Times* and *The Guardian*

(IBT 2012, 8). Izama explained that he had been asked to write a blog so that he could be quoted, and that 'this thing acquired a life of its own' (Chalk 2012, 8). African voices have historically been silenced in international coverage of Africa (Hawk 1992). In the case of *Kony2012*, however, the international media did attempt to include some of these voices, and this was enabled by the social media.

Reactions to the video in Uganda, were also discussed in the international media. CNTV, among others, reported on screenings of the movie which provoked a furious response in the Lira district.[3] Similarly, *The Guardian* started its live feed with Polly Curtis (2012) writing: 'Our principle [sic] approach is to attempt to gather views from Uganda about whether this film is the right way to go about campaigning on the issue.' Al Jazeera went further by providing one of the most sophisticated attempts at including local voices,[4] through the use of social media. Their page 'Uganda speaks' (2012) called for local contributions via email, SMS or tweets:

> The rest of the world has had their say, and now Al Jazeera wants to hear voices from inside Uganda. What do you think about the situation and what solutions do you have to share with the international community?

They created an interactive map reflecting comments from within Uganda. Reactions were categorised, with some 55 per cent being against the campaign, 30 per cent supporting it and 15 per cent remaining neutral. This constitutes a strong initiative by a major (but non-Western) international news organisation to include voices historically silenced in mainstream media coverage of Africa.

More generally, international news organisations tried to capitalise on the global awareness and to recontextualise the conflict, using previous reports or interviewing journalists who had covered the conflict. Panorama, the flagship BBC programme in investigative journalism, broadcast a 30-minute documentary by Sierra Leonean Bafta-winning reporter, Sorious Samusa (2012). It followed up on the current 'hunt' for Kony, providing an historical analysis of the conflict, and interviews with victims of the LRA and former LRA commander Kenneth Banya, thus shifting the focus from the video to the issue itself. Another example of coverage challenging a one-sided understanding of *Kony2012* was the video produced by *The Guardian*, which captures the reactions of children from London. In doing so, it addressed the various and contradictory ways in which the video was perceived, even by an audience of Western youths.

The various frames detailed above suggest that the international media not only covered the video and its backlash, but also tried to remediate some of the video's flaws. Even more, it forced some journalists to reflect on the failure of the international media to raise the profile of the LRA conflict earlier. Reiz (2010) compared the coverage of the conflict from 2004 to 2008 across the *Times*, *The Guardian*, *The Mail and Guardian* and *The Daily Monitor*. Her analysis demonstrates a general lack of coverage of the conflict, in international periodicals in particular. At its peak, 52 articles were published in August 2006 during the Juba peace talks, with 40 articles appearing in *The Monitor*. This is obviously in sharp contrast to the tremendous awareness raised by the IC video. Hence, journalists Roger Cohen and Pulitzer Prize-winner Nicholas Kristof supported the fact that the video, in Green's (2012) words, 'achieved more with (a) 30 minute video than battalions of diplomats, NGO workers and journalists have since the conflict began 26 years ago'. Barbara Among (in Chalk 2012, 5), editor of Ugandan newspaper *The Daily Monitor*, explains: 'The good thing is that it has raised awareness outside of Uganda. [...] The impact this has created is bigger than the impact my stories created for 8 years.' Beyond an ethic of pragmatism, these reactions suggest reflexivity on the part of journalists *within* the media coverage. Live on CNN, international correspondent Amanpour (2012) celebrated this awareness which the journalists had not managed to raise, while acknowledging the limits of the video. Similarly, Lindsey Hilsum (2012), experienced foreign correspondent and international editor of Channel 4, wrote:

> None of the articles … I or a hundred other journalists who have covered Uganda over 25 years has reached the people this video has reached. Ok, it may not be accurate. It may use out-of-date figures. But it's struck a chord we have never managed to strike. [...] The 'Invisible Children' campaign could learn a little from those of us who care about accuracy and context. But I think we could learn something from them about how to get a message across, and how to talk to a generation that has stopped bothering to read newspaper and watch TV news.

Becket (2012a, 6) argues that Hilsum's ambivalence about a 'human right projects which had achieved dramatic impact but with debatable means and aims' constituted a thread underlying all the international coverage. That such reflexivity on the part of journalists emerged within the coverage is assuredly worth researching further, but for now we can highlight an apparent limit to such reflexivity. As noted above, many critics (including journalists) attacked the colonial tone of the video. In fact, it could be argued that the video was so successful precisely because it tapped into a narcissistic, simplistic and reassuring Western narrative about Africa. Yet (and despite discussing this), journalists possibly failed to address a broader issue, namely the historical role of the international media in sustaining and fostering this same cultural background against which the *Kony2012* video was set.

Covering *Kony2012* constituted nothing short of a jigsaw puzzle, and the international media used many frames to do so, from the 'Internet sensation' to criticisms of the timing and policy of the campaign, the simplification of the situation, and the colonial undertones of the video. It will take more research to understand in-depth the differences in coverage across media organisations, both internationally and locally. The way journalists relied on social media to cover the story, and the extent to which this opens up the space to provide more innovative and disruptive coverage, also deserve critical attention. For now, this example has shown three ways in which the social media impacted mainstream reporting; it allowed for an immediate integration of the backlash into the coverage so as to partly include African voices; and, to an extent, it forced media organisations to be reflexive.

Notes

1   http://blogs.independent.co.uk/2012/03/07/stop-kony-yes-but-dont-stop-asking-questions/

2   As can clearly be seen at the end of the video where American youth are seen taking over the streets, uplifted by upbeat dub step music.

3   http://english.cntv.cn/program/newsupdate/20120319/106930.shtml

4   It should be noted, however, that such initiative remains limited in that it potentially favours the views of urban elites with a stronger access to technology. See, for instance, the International Broadcasting Trust report by Chalk (2012) for a summary of Internet access and media usage in Uganda.

References

Amanpour, C. 2012. *CNN*, 9 March. http://edition.cnn.com/video/?iid=article_sidebar#/video/world/2012/03/09/uganda-kony-film-amanpour-reax.cnn (accessed 29 January 2013).

Beckett, C. 2012a. Communicating for change: Media and agency in the networked public sphere. POLIS, London School of Economics and Political Science. http://www2.lse.ac.uk/media@lse/POLIS/documents/Communicating-For-Change-.pdf (accessed 29 January 2013).

Beckett, C. 2012b. Why I think the Kony 2012 campaign is wrong. POLIS, 9 March. http://blogs.lse.ac.uk/polis/2012/03/09/why-i-think-the-kony-2012-campaign-is-wrong/ (accessed 29 January 2013).

Branch, A. 2012. Dangerous ignorance: The hysteria of Kony2012. *Al Jazeera*, 12 March. http://www.aljazeera.com/indepth/opinion/2012/03/201231284336601364.html (accessed 29 January 2013).

Chalk, S. 2012. Kony2012: Success or failure? International Broadcasting Trust. http://www.ibt.org.uk/all_documents/research/IBT_KonySOweb.pdf (accessed 29 January 2013).

Chouliaraki, L. 2012. *The ironic spectator: Solidarity in the age of post-humanitarianism.* Cambridge: Polity.

Curtis, P. and T. McCarthy. 2012. Kony2012: What's the real story? *The Guardian*, 8 March. http://www.guardian.co.uk/politics/reality-check-with-polly-curtis/2012/mar/08/kony-2012-what-s-the-story (accessed 29 January 2013).

Dupuis, A. 2012. Stop Joseph Kony. *France24*, 8 March. http://www.france24.com/en/20120307-2012-03-07-2220-wb-en-media-watch (accessed 29 January 2013).

Green, M. 2012. Let the Kony campaign be just the start. *Financial Times*, 12 March. http://www.ft.com/cms/s/0/882c6c6a-6c34-11e1-8c9d-00144feab49a.html#axzz2JO1YeEz6 (accessed 29 January 2013).

Izama, A. 2012. Acholi Street. Stop #Kony2012. Invisible Children's campaign of infamy, 7 March. http://angeloizama.com/2012/03/07 (accessed 29 January 2013).

Kagumire, R. 2012. My response to KONY2012. YouTube, 7 March. http://www.youtube.com/watch?v=KLVY5jBnD-E (accessed 29 January 2013).

Mckenzie, D. 2012. 'KONY 2012' viral video raises questions about filmmakers. *CNN*, 12 March. http://edition.cnn.com/2012/03/09/world/africa/kony-2012-q-and-a/index.html (accessed 29 January 2013).

Orgeret, K. 2010. Mediated culture and the well-informed global citizen: Images of Africa in the Global North. *Nordicom Review* 2: 47–61.

Oyston, G. 2012. Visible children. http://visiblechildren.tumblr.com/ (accessed 29 January 2013).

Reiz, N. 2010. War in the North? A critical study of news coverage of the Lord's Resistance Army 2004–2008. Master's thesis, University of Kansas. http://kuscholarworks.ku.edu/dspace/bitstream/1808/7636/1/Reiz_ku_0099M_11196_DATA_1.pdf (accessed 29 January 2013).

Rourke, A. 2012. Joseph Kony documentary makes move from social media to mainstream TV. *The Guardian*, 8 March. http://www.guardian.co.uk/world/2012/mar/08/joseph-kony-social-media-tv (accessed 29 January 2013).

Samusa, S. 2012. Kony: Hunt for the world's most wanted. *BBC Panorama*, 20 August.

Wilkerson, M. 2012. Guest post: Joseph Kony is not in Uganda (and other complicated things). *Foreign Policy*, 7 March. http://blog.foreignpolicy.com/posts/2012/03/07/guest_post_joseph_kony_is_not_in_uganda_and_other_complicated_things (accessed 29 January 2013).

Index